D0515886

THE NBA
TODAY'S STARS
TOMORROW'S LEGENDS

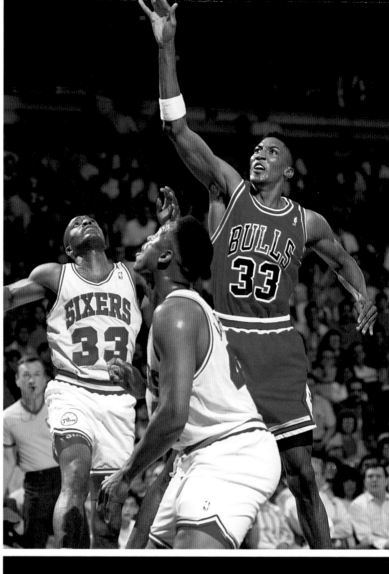

THE NBA
TODAY'S STARS
TOMORROW'S LEGENDS

JACK CLARY

Brompton

First published in 1993 by
Brompton Books Corp.
15 Sherwood Place
Greenwich, Connecticut 06830
USA

ISBN 1-85841-095-9

Printed in China

This edition is revised and updated.

Reprinted 1994, 1996

Page 1: *Michael Jordan is back and better than ever. In 1996 he led the Chicago Bulls to a fourth NBA Championship.*

Page 2: *Clockwise: Patrick Ewing, Scottie Pippen, David Robinson and Karl Malone.*

Below: *Shaquille O'Neal has become an almost unstoppable force at center.*

CONTENTS

INTRODUCTION

In some ways professional basketball is like Old Man River – it just keeps rollin' along, from year to year, from generation to generation. Exceptional players define the scope of the hoop sport, establishing new records of excellence that stand only until they are broken by the next rising star.

Michael Jordan tried to convey that message when he announced his retirement before the 1994 season by noting that there are other great players such as Charles Barkley, David Robinson, Hakeem Olajuwon, Patrick Ewing and Shaquille O'Neal already performing in the NBA, and that there are some potential pro greats in college or even in high school, who will some day step forward and be stars of the same magnitude as he had been. At the same time, he also left open the door for his own return – and in March 1995 he was back in a Bulls uniform. A year later he led Chicago to its fourth NBA title in six years. He also proved that while there are many great players in the NBA, he is still the best.

This volume focuses on those NBA stars who are at the beginning or pinnacle of their careers, many of whom will take the sport to new heights into the new millennium, and who are destined to become the basketball legends of tomorrow. The pantheon of stars includes such well-known players as Karl Malone, Tim Hardaway, Shawn Kemp, Scottie Pippen and John Stockton, as well as Jordan, Barkley, Larry Johnson, Robinson, Olajuwon,

Left: *Michael Jordan, seen here soaring to a second Olympic gold medal in 1992, returned to the NBA in 1995 after a brief retirement and led Chicago to an NBA title the following season.*

Above: *Shaquille O'Neal was the NBA's Number 1 draft choice in the 1993 season, which culminated with his selection as Rookie of the Year. He went from the Magic to the Lakers after the 1996 season.*

Ewing and O'Neal. More recently, such new stars as Kenny Anderson, Alonzo Mourning, Jamal Mashburn, Glen Rice, Jim Jackson, Anfernee Hardaway, John Starks, Isaiah Rider, Latrell Sprewell and Gary Payton have begun to make their mark on the NBA.

Today's masterful athletes of the court, with their grace, coordination and strength, often are compared to such great ballet masters as Mikhail Baryshnikov. Excessive hyperbole? Perhaps . . . unless one has watched Michael Jordan and his endless array of airborne antics in which he seems to go several directions at once while on an extemporaneous flight to the basket . . . or has marveled at the elegant movements of 7' 1" David Robinson underneath the basket, when he either slams home a dunk shot or leaps, like a striking snake, to block a shot. Those leaps and dunks are both born of talent and hard work, and are as inspiring for those on the court as for those in the stands. These men are a joy to watch.

Basketball now more than ever is a sport of great stars, many of whom are more athletic and swift than their predecessors of 20 or 30 years ago were, and who can shoot better from positions once deemed only the orchestrated province of the famed Harlem Globetrotters. Their basic basketball skills elegantly complement astounding athletic grace and strength.

San Antonio's David Robinson was Rookie of the Year in 1990 and the NBA's MVP in 1995. He has become both a great scorer and rebounder. Many also believe that Alonzo Mourning, center for the Miami Heat, will be the equal of O'Neal when he finally gains experience. With Larry Johnson, the NBA's 1992 Rookie of the Year, Mourning took his old Charlotte team into the playoffs for the first time ever in his 1993 rookie season. Everyone agrees that he can be a dominating inside player following in the footsteps of Patrick Ewing.

A number of other new players are seeking to make an impact in the NBA such as Jim Jackson, Jamal Mashburn, Anfernee Hardaway, Isaiah (J.R.) Rider, Clarence Weatherspoon, Chris Webber, Gary Payton and Latrell Sprewell.

Jim Jackson gave up his last year of eligibility to join the NBA in the 1992 draft. But his ability to direct an offense with his great ballhandling and passing skills, and a deadly outside jump, set him apart from every other guard during his final two college seasons.

Jamal Mashburn is considered one of the best small forwards to come into the NBA in many years. At 6' 8", he can also play at guard in the mold of Magic Johnson. He was the bulwark of Kentucky's NCAA tourney teams, and he has picked up where he left off in college with his all-around play that has been a perfect complement to Jim Jackson's great talent.

Anfernee "Penny" Hardaway of the Orlando Magic, a 6' 7" point guard, is also compared to Magic Johnson. In 1995, he helped take the Magic to the NBA Finals, and

Above: *Juwon Howard caught fire as one of the NBA's rising young stars during his second year with the Washington Bullets when he passed the 2,500-point mark. He was traded to Miami in 1996.*

Right: *Some wondered if Jason Kidd made an error by leaving college after his sophomore year to become a top round draft pick of the Mavericks. In 1996, he was the first Dallas player ever named an All-Star Game starter.*

While many of the stars featured in this volume are about to reach the peak of their careers, or are on the steep ascendancy curve to stardom, there are others who quietly became stars in the early 1990s – players such as Kevin Johnson of Phoenix; Detroit's Joe Dumars; Detlef Schrempf of Seattle; ex-Olympian Clyde Drexler; and Hakeem Olajuwon, who led the Houston Rockets to the 1994 and 1995 NBA title. But the NBA is a world of ever-changing stars, and those who hit the heights in the 1990s promise to dominate the game right to the millennium.

Certainly, Shaquille O'Neal has been the game's most visible player. He is a young multi-millionaire whose name and face are connected with so many product endorsements that it is difficult to go a day without seeing or hearing about the "Shaq Attack." He was the 1993 Rookie of the Year, and a year later, helped by two other new talented stars, Anfernee Hardaway and Nick Anderson, he led the Magic into the NBA Finals. He is 7' 1", over 300 pounds and his offensive skills are still being polished. But his presence on the court is never in doubt, and many have compared him to Wilt Chamberlain, one of the greatest centers ever to play on the NBA courts.

While O'Neal may be the NBA's most talked-about player, there are several other stars who are in his class.

he was selected to the All-NBA first team in both 1995 and 1996. Hardaway's forte is his flexibility, because he also can play small forward.

Isaiah Rider has often been compared to Mitch Richmond, Sacramento's fine shooting guard. He is a flamboyant player, but that part of his game has yet to be fully appreciated because the Minnesota Timberwolves are still struggling to become respectable. (He was traded to Portland at the end of the 1996 season.) At 6' 5", he averaged more than 29 points per game in the second of his two seasons at University of Nevada-Las Vegas.

Clarence Weatherspoon is a "do-it-all" player who has played at both forward positions, and even at center, though he is just 6' 7". He came into the NBA with credentials supporting his defensive skills – and he still guards the opposition's best scorer – but he also has enlarged his scoring talent, and is rewriting many of the Philadelphia 76ers' records.

Chris Webber was the Golden State Warriors' top pick in the 1994 season, and he won the Rookie of the Year award. But he showed the immaturity that often comes when a player leaves college too early for the pros, and he began wrangling with his coach, Don Nelson, eventually leading him to be traded to the Washington Bullets where it is hoped he can duplicate his rookie performances. At 6' 9" and 245 pounds, he is the prototype power forward. He has great hands and his offense has begun to rise to the levels many have predicted, with flashes of brilliance as his playing time increases. He also

is a tough rebounder, and most NBA observers believe that once he finally settles down and accepts the rigors and discipline of the NBA, he will be a fine player.

Both Gary Payton and Latrell Sprewell have made their mark rather quickly, and without much fanfare because neither came into the NBA with all the gloss and glitter that accompanied players such as O'Neal and Webber.

Payton, a member of the Seattle Supersonics, was college basketball's Player of the Year in 1990, playing at Oregon State University. He has methodically worked to improve his game, and by his fifth season he was a solid choice for the All-NBA team and All-Star team. He also had accumulated more than 1,000 assists by that time and more than 600 steals in his role of running Seattle's offense – one that helped the Sonics to the NBA's best record in 1994 and to the NBA Finals in 1996.

Sprewell has seemingly arrived at the top faster than Payton. The 6' 5" guard from Alabama was a first round pick in 1992 and he got a spot on the All-NBA team after just two seasons, during which he had begun to rewrite the Warriors' scoring records. Both players have one common attribute: They are indefatigable, never missing a game and averaging nearly 40 minutes in those they play.

Christian Laettner and Shawn Bradley were college stars in the early 1990s who are on their way up and are on the brink of cracking the NBA's top echelon.

Christian Laettner was a great college player whose coolness under fire was best exemplified by his dramatic last-second turnaround winning jump shot against the University of Kentucky in the NCAA semi-final championships in 1992 that propelled Duke to the finals; and in his dramatic second-half performance in the finals against Michigan that enabled the Blue Devils to win their second straight collegiate title. He was the only collegian selected for the U.S. Olympic team in 1992. There followed great expectations for him with the Minnesota Timberwolves but they never materialized and he was traded to the Atlanta Hawks, where a much more solid team should benefit him. Yet, there have been many times when the 6' 11", 225-pound power forward has shown his great talent, and he still is fired by a physical and mental toughness.

Shawn Bradley, a giant at 7' 6" who played at Brigham Young, is the most intriguing new player in the NBA because he played only one season at BYU and not at all in 1992 or 1993 while fulfilling his agreement to be a Mormon missionary in Australia. However, some NBA scouts call him "a once in a lifetime player," someone a team can build around, much as Orlando is doing with O'Neal. Bradley still is considered something of a project because of his limited college experience and his need to bulk up his 250-pound frame so he can take the pounding from bigger centers like O'Neal, Olajuwon, Robinson and Ewing.

There are also two fine European players who made their debut in the NBA during the 1990s – Toni Kukoc, a 6' 10" forward-guard who was considered Europe's best player when he signed with the Chicago Bulls; and Boston's Dino Radja, a 6' 10" forward who tries to stabilize this storied franchise as it rebuilds. Kukoc has the

good fortune to meld his talents with Michael Jordan and has begun to assimilate to both a higher level of competition and to the cultural differences of playing and living in the United States.

And there are newcomers like Jason Kidd of Dallas; Juwon Howard of the Miami Heat, who vied with Grant Hill to be 1995 Rookie of the Year; the Milwaukee Bucks' Glenn Robinson, the 1994 College Player of the Year; and Eric Montross of Dallas.

And for good measure keep an eye on Atlanta's Mookie Blaylock and Detroit's Stacy Augmon; Nick Van Exel of the Lakers, who made the NBA's All-Rookie team in 1994; and Cedric Ceballos of the Los Angeles Lakers. Ceballos played four seasons at Phoenix and hit his stride in his final two years before moving to the Lakers.

There may be others to watch: Calbert Cheaney of the Bullets; Denver's Rodney Rogers; Loy Vaught and Lamond Murray of the Los Angeles Clippers; Terrell Brandon of Cleveland; Allan Houston of New York; and youngsters Jerry Stackhouse of Philadelphia, and Damon Stoudamire, who is becoming a budding star for the expansion Toronto Raptors. In the 1997 season, they were joined by All-Americas Marcus Camby, Antoine Walker, John Wallace, Eric Dampier, Shareef Abdur-Rahim and Ray Allen.

As these rising stars join the ranks of the NBA's greatest players, and as today's heroes become tomorrow's legends, the NBA will continue to attract additional millions of fans here and abroad. The star players who make a difference – to their teams, their fans and in the record books – create the colorful legacy of pro basketball. And that is what the NBA is about.

Right: *As a rookie in 1996, Jerry Stackhouse was like a breath of fresh air for the Philadelphia 76ers. He set 76ers rookie records in scoring, minutes played and foul throws attempted and made. He also led all NBA rookies in scoring with nearly 20 points per game.*

KENNY ANDERSON

Position: Guard
College: Georgia Tech
Drafted: New Jersey, Ist Rd. ('91)

Birth Date: Oct. 9, 1970
Height: 6' 1"
Weight: 170

Kenny Anderson is following the same path to NBA point guard stardom as former Detroit star Isiah Thomas. Like Thomas, Anderson had only two years of college experience when he came into the NBA, and his rivals immediately likened him to the Pistons All-Star, who once led his team to a pair of NBA titles.

"He's going to be one of the premier point guards in the league," notes one of his fiercest rivals, guard John Starks of the New York Knicks. "He's in the class of Isiah Thomas and Magic Johnson. There's no question he has all the skills that they had. He runs the team. He passes the ball well. He's like Isiah the way he pushes it up and down the court."

Though he averaged more than 23 points a game during his two seasons at Georgia Tech, Anderson had a rough start in the NBA with the New Jersey Nets. He missed his rookie training camp and joined the team after the season had begun, and started just 13 games. Still, he led his team in assists 17 times and in steals 10 times in his substitute role.

Anderson proved his talent in his second season, taking over control of the Nets' offense and forging a 17-point scoring average. He was sidelined two-thirds of the way into the season with a broken wrist.

Ken reached All-Star status in his third season, starting for the Eastern Conference team. He led all NBA point guards in scoring and set the Nets' all-time assists record during the 1995 season. He was traded to Charlotte in 1996 and became the Hornets' point guard. He finished among the NBA's top ten assists leaders.

Left: *Kenny Anderson has become one of the NBA's best young playmakers. He set a career assists record for the Nets in 1995. In his first season with Charlotte he had 17 10+ assist games and 15 double-doubles in just 38 games.*

NICK ANDERSON

Right: *Nick Anderson optioned to leave college a year early and became the first player drafted by Orlando – and now is the last one left from the Magic's first team in 1989. He has used the fine rebounding and defensive skills he'd honed at the University of Illinois to create a better all-around game in the NBA.*

Position: Guard
College: Illinois
Drafted: Orlando, 1st Rd. ('89)

Birth Date: Jan. 20, 1968
Height: 6' 6"
Weight: 215

Nick Anderson surprised many in the NBA when he opted to forego his final year of college eligibility at the University of Illinois and tossed his name into the 1989 draft. The Orlando Magic have been delighted. He has been a perfect fit with the Magic's strong four-guard rotation in teaming with Penny Hardaway, Brian Shaw and Dennis Scott. While he still is a key performer in Orlando's role as a title contender, he no longer has the burden of being the Magic's top backcourt scorer as was the case during his pre-Shaquille O'Neal seasons with the Magic, when he was the team's top scorer.

With his steady production climb and his solid all-around play, Anderson has fulfilled all that the Magic had hoped he could provide. For example, in his rookie season he averaged 11.5 points per game, but by his sixth year, he averaged 16. He has accumulated more than 2,000 rebounds and 1,000 assists. His defense also improved: he has averaged 120 steals a year. With his fine athletic skills, he gained a reputation as a shot-blocker, averaging 40 per season. Nick complements his skills with a good three-point shooting touch. In 1996, he tied a club single-game record with nine three-pointers against the Utah Jazz.

Anderson is a powerfully-built player, reminding many of the perennial All-Star Clyde Drexler. That strength, combined with a "nose" for the ball, has helped with his rebounding.

Former Orlando Magic coach and TV commentator Matt Goukas comments, "With a stronger team around him, he has become one of the elite players in the NBA."

CHARLES BARKLEY

Position: Forward   **Birth Date:** Feb. 20, 1963
College: Auburn   **Height:** 6' 6"
Drafted: Philadelphia, 1st. Rd. ('84)   **Weight:** 252

Charles Barkley has never been at a loss for words – about himself, his team, your team, his owner and fans, and anything else that strikes his fancy.

He also has never been found wanting on the basketball court, where he presents an awesome sight as he comes roaring down the floor, looking all the while like a rhino out of control. And that is how defenders in the NBA treat him – deliberately staying out of his way when he is cruising in to the basket.

That was one of the key reasons why Barkley was chosen the NBA's MVP for the 1993 season, as he led the Phoenix Suns to the Western Conference championship in just his first season after being traded from Philadelphia, where he played for seven years.

Barkley is one of the most unusual players in the sport's history, and not because of his size. But it is his size that calls attention to all that he does. Former Celtics star Kevin McHale, who waged some classic battles against Barkley for over a half dozen seasons, said, "No one in the game is stronger."

Barkley looks more like a pro football lineman than an NBA forward, yet he has the grace and athleticism of a player 30 or 40 pounds lighter, and a few inches smaller. His size causes teams tremendous problems in trying to match up.

Unlike some very big players whose main job is to clog the middle and try to keep opposing rebounders away, Barkley has a deft shooting touch. He ranks among the

Left: *Charles Barkley is one of the NBA's most colorful players, who backs up much of his outrageousness with some great playing skills that earned him the NBA's MVP award in 1993 and a spot on two U.S. Olympic basketball teams.*

Opposite: *In 1996, Barkley became the 10th NBA player to pass the 20,000 points-10,000 rebounds plateau.*

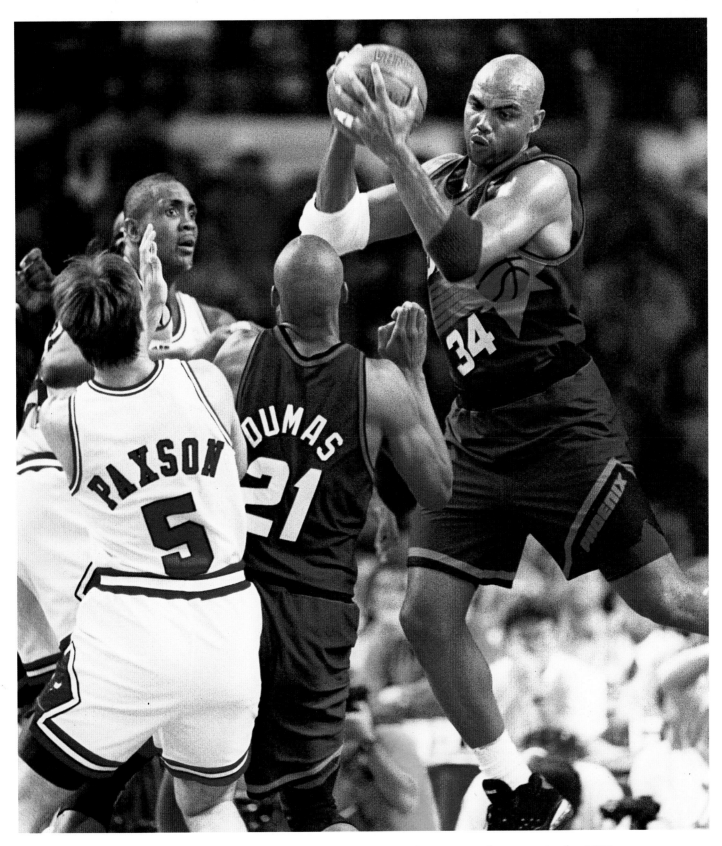

Opposite: *With the 76ers, Barkley averaged 12 rebounds a game to complement his scoring.*

Above: *Barkley often seems like a one-man gang on the court.*

top five all-time 76ers scorers, and has led Phoenix every season.

He also has become a force around the boards with his rebounds, averaging more than 800 per season.

He has been a regular on the NBA All-Star team, and he was selected as the game's MVP in 1991 after pulling down 22 rebounds – the most since Wilt Chamberlain's record-setting performance in the 1967 game.

Barkley was the fourth all-time scorer at Auburn where he left a year early to play in the NBA, and was later picked as the Southeast Conference's Player of the Decade of the Eighties. He was cut by coach Bobby Knight late in the 1984 U.S. Olympic trials ("He did me a great favor because I found out what it takes to compete at a higher level"), but was named to America's team for the 1992 Olympic Games at Barcelona, and became its most notable performer both on and off the court. He also was a member of Dream Team III at the 1996 Games in Atlanta.

MOOKIE BLAYLOCK

Position: Guard
College: Oklahoma
Drafted: New Jersey, 1st Rd. ('89)

Birth Date: Mar. 20, 1967
Height: 6' 1"
Weight: 185

Mention Daron Oashay Blaylock and few will recognize the name. Mention Mookie Blaylock, and NBA fans will know immediately that you are referring to the lightning-quick guard of the Atlanta Hawks – one of the league's best defensive players who has annually been among its leaders in steals and assists.

Blaylock played for the first three years of his career with the New Jersey Nets after setting the NCAA single season record for steals in his first year at Oklahoma. After

the Nets chose Ken Anderson in the draft in 1991, they sent Blaylock and forward Roy Hinson to the Atlanta Hawks in a trade for guard Rumeal Robinson just before the start of the 1992 season.

Blaylock, who has combined with Stacy Augmon to give Atlanta one of the league's best backcourt tandems, has supplied the direction for the Hawks to win the division title in 1996. He is a regular on the NBA All-Defensive teams. In 1996, he tied his team's record with 212 steals and finished second in the NBA. That year the Hawks were 19-9 when he played 40+ minutes, and 17-9 when he shot .500+. Mookie has accumulated more than 3,000 assists and 1,000 steals.

Left: *Guard Mookie Blaylock has elevated his game to All-Star dimensions in Atlanta. He was selected to the NBA All-Defensive first team in 1994, and in 1995 he added four points per game to his previous totals.*

Opposite: *Cedric Ceballos went from the Phoenix Suns to the Los Angeles Lakers in 1995 as a free agent, and he immediately stepped in to fill the void left by the retirement of perennial All-Star forward James Worthy by leading the team in scoring in 1995 and 1996.*

CEDRIC CEBALLOS

Position: Forward
College: Cal-State (Fullerton)
Drafted: Phoenix, 2nd Rd. ('90)

Birth Date: Aug. 2, 1969
Height: 6' 7"
Weight: 225

Cedric Ceballos got caught up in a numbers game with the Phoenix Suns – they had too many talented forwards prior to the 1995 season – and he found himself with no place to go but the Los Angeles Lakers. There, Ceballos found a team desperately needing a scoring forward following the retirement of James Worthy. He filled the vacancy immediately, and in the 1995 and 1996 seasons he became the first Laker to average 20+ points in back-to-back seasons since Worthy did it in 1990-1991.

In his final season in Phoenix, Ceballos averaged more than 19 points per game playing on a team where Charles Barkley was the go-to guy. He had been the NBA's most accurate field goal shooter during the 1993 season, averaging nearly 58 percent.

Ceballos, who is a native of the Hawaiian island of Maui, has continued on an upward track through his NBA career. He was just the player the once-upon-a-time showtime Lakers needed, because he won the NBA's Slam Dunk Championship in 1992 and plays at a high level of intensity. With the Lakers, he also became a big factor on the boards, averaging more than two rebounds a game more than during his four seasons in Phoenix.

DERRICK COLEMAN

Position: Forward
College: Syracuse
Drafted: New Jersey, 1st Rd. ('90)

Birth Date: June 21, 1967
Height: 6' 10"
Weight: 230

Derrick Coleman was a collegiate legend when he came into the NBA as its first pick of the 1990 draft.

As a four-year starter at Syracuse, he became the NCAA's all-time rebound leader with a total of 1,537; and he is recognized as the first player ever to score 2,000 points, grab 1,500 rebounds and block 300 shots in a career.

Coleman was traded to the Philadelphia 76ers during the 1996 season after spending his first five seasons with the New Jersey Nets. He made an immediate impact with the 76ers, recording double-doubles in his first two games. He was the first 76ers player in 1996 to lead the team in points, assists and rebounds in the same game.

Coleman was a top draft pick of the Nets and was named Rookie of the Year in 1991. Coleman was also the Nets' all-time leader in scoring and rebounding. He was a starter for the Eastern Conference in the 1994 All-Star Game and he has never averaged fewer than 18 points per game during his entire NBA career.

Right: *Derrick Coleman won NBA Rookie of the Year honors in 1991 after averaging more than 18 points per game and pulling down 759 rebounds. He was a member of the U.S. Dream Team II that won the World Championship in 1994.*

CLYDE DREXLER

Position: Guard   **Birth Date:** June 22, 1962
College: University of Houston   **Height:** 6' 7"
Drafted: Portland, 1st Rd. ('83)   **Weight:** 222

Many in the NBA claim that if Clyde Drexler played in New York, Los Angeles or Chicago, he would be among the league's five most popular players. Instead, he played in Portland, Oregon, the NBA's smallest market, until being traded to Houston in 1995.

He is Portland's all-time leader in eight of 10 major statistical areas (all but three-point shots attempted and made), a perennial All-Star Game participant and the go-to guy when things are tough. In short, he was the principal reason why the Trail Blazers became a force in the Western Division early in the 1990s.

Drexler came into the NBA with some good credentials – a member of the University of Houston's rollicking "Phi Slama Jama" teams that made racehorse basketball a way of life en route to consecutive trips to

Above: *Drexler has been named to nine NBA All-Star teams and led Portland to the playoffs during his first eleven NBA seasons.*

Left: *Clyde Drexler, who was Portland's all-time leader in eight of ten major categories, joined the NBA champion Houston Rockets during the 1995 season and immediately added speed and scoring power to their backcourt.*

the NCAA Final Four. Those credentials along with his athleticism were impressive, but when he came into the NBA some believed him to be an incomplete player, questioning his passing and ballhandling skills, his outside shooting and his durability. His Blazer teammates looked to him for offense, and that mainly consisted of his ability to drive to the basket. But when Drexler refined his outside shooting, it became a perfect foil against defenders overplaying his drives. The quintessential team player was in his element, and he was rewarded by being selected to the U.S. Olympic basketball "Dream Team" in 1992.

Clyde thrives on pressure; self confidence has never been a problem for him. "If you don't believe in yourself, who else is going to believe in you?" he asks.

Clyde reached the apex of his career when after being traded to the Houston Rockets during the 1995 season, he was reunited with his old college teammate Hakeem Olajuwon, and they took the Rockets to a second straight NBA title.

Above right: *No guard in the NBA is faster afoot than Drexler, who is renowned for his explosive end-to-end drives. He played a key role in helping Houston to the 1995 NBA title.*

Right: *Clyde Drexler participates in the 1992 All-Star Game. Drexler's game has grown to the point where, though playing guard, he has accumulated more rebounds than assists.*

20

JOE DUMARS

Position: Guard
College: McNeese State
Drafted: Detroit, 1st Rd. ('85)

Birth Date: May 24, 1963
Height: 6' 3"
Weight: 190

When the Detroit Pistons were among the NBA's elite in the late eighties and early nineties – culminating with back-to-back titles in 1989 and 1990 – their most underrated player was Joe Dumars. He also was their most valuable player.

Even with the Pistons' halycon championship years apparently behind them, Dumars continues to apply leadership and consistent production. He was selected as MVP in Detroit's first world championship victory; received a fair bit of notoriety when named to four consecutive NBA All-Star teams in 1990-1993; and led the team in scoring for four straight seasons (1991-1994). More important to him were his four-time first team selections to the league's All-Defensive team.

"Fans probably were never aware of what Joe really was doing until the game was over and everything fell into place," noted former Detroit coach Chuck Daly. "We never judged his performances by box score numbers, but he was like the glue that held us together in tough spots. . . . Joe was steady, unrelenting, and when we asked him to take on the other team's big scoring guard, he always gave us a good game."

Many in the NBA say that Dumars' true value has been

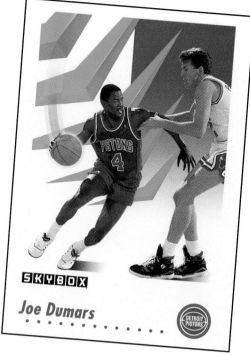

Above: *Joe Dumars played on two Detroit NBA championship teams in 1989-90, and was playoff MVP in 1989.*

Below: *Dumars has been on the All-Defensive first team four times, and has led Detroit in scoring four times.*

his continued high level of play on a team that has undergone coaching changes and is being remade after its championship years. In 1993, his 23.5 points-per-game scoring average was the highest of his career as he stepped forward to take the on-the-court offensive. He also averaged more than 40 minutes a game, further underscoring how much the Pistons have come to rely on his direction.

Above: *Joe Dumars was an underrated player when he was a member of the Detroit Pistons' NBA championship teams in the late 1980s, but with the departure of some of the team's stars he has recently become the team's top point-maker. A first round pick in 1985 from McNeese State University, he now ranks fourth among all-time Detroit scorers and third in steals and assists.*

SEAN ELLIOTT

Left: *Sean Elliott was the third player selected in the 1989 draft as a lottery pick by San Antonio, after playing four seasons at the University of Arizona where he finished as the Pac-10's all-time scorer.*

Below: *The Spurs won nearly 75 percent of its games when Elliott scored 20 or more points. He led the Spurs in foul shooting accuracy during his first three seasons. Elliott was traded by the Spurs for Dennis Rodman after the 1993 season. His career was in jeopardy after an injured knee voided a trade to Houston for Robert Horry. He spent two seasons with the Pistons and then returned to San Antonio in 1995.*

Position: Forward
College: Arizona
Drafted: San Antonio, 1st Rd. ('89)

Birth Date: Feb. 2, 1968
Height: 6' 8"
Weight: 215

Sean Elliott has a clear view of his role as a player. During his first stint with the San Antonio Spurs, he said, "Our big guns have always been Terry Cummings and David Robinson and I am there to support them. If either one isn't on, I'm fully capable of picking it up."

And how. The 6' 8" forward quickly became a major force in the Spurs' offense and defense, and he did the same with the Detroit Pistons before returning to San Antonio.

Elliott was college basketball's Player of the Year in 1989, but it wasn't until the 1996 season that he reached the levels long predicted for him in the NBA. He averaged 20 points per game, led the team in scoring 24 times, became the Spurs' all-time career three-point scorer and played in his second All-Star Game.

PATRICK EWING

Position: Center	**Birth Date:** Aug. 5, 1962
College: Georgetown	**Height:** 7' 0"
Drafted: New York, 1st Rd. ('85)	**Weight:** 240

"Do what it takes to win." That is the first and foremost commandment in Patrick Ewing's lexicon of basic basketball rules. And since entering the NBA as the first "lottery" pick in 1985, he has tried valiantly to adhere to that idea.

It hasn't always been easy, because he has had nine coaches during his time with the Knicks, and the lack of stability that any player needs – even great ones like him – sapped his ability to produce championships.

Still, he is one of the most dominating centers in the NBA. The seven-foot native of Jamaica was a schoolboy sensation in Cambridge, Massachusetts, and attracted scholarship offers from over 300 colleges. He chose Georgetown University in Washington, and led the Hoyas to three appearances in the NCAA championship game.

While in college, Ewing also won the first of his two Olympic gold medals, as a member of the 1984 U.S. team. He also was a member of the 1992 U.S. Dream Team in Barcelona, and used that performance as a springboard for the 1993 season in which he led the Knicks to the Eastern Division championship. In 1994 he led them to the NBA Finals.

Above: *Patrick Ewing was the No.1 draft pick in the NBA in 1985 by the New York Knicks and has been the team's starting center since the first game of his pro career.*

Right: *Ewing is the only Knick ever to score 2,000 points in more than one season, and led the Knicks in scoring every season. Renowned for his thunderous dunks, he has learned how to control his game, and blend his scoring and his defense into one hard-nosed and aggressive package.*

Opposite: *In college Ewing played in three NCAA championship games, helping his Georgetown team to the title in 1984. As a collegian he also won a gold medal with the U.S. Olympic team. Ewing was a member of the 1992 U.S. Olympic team as well.*

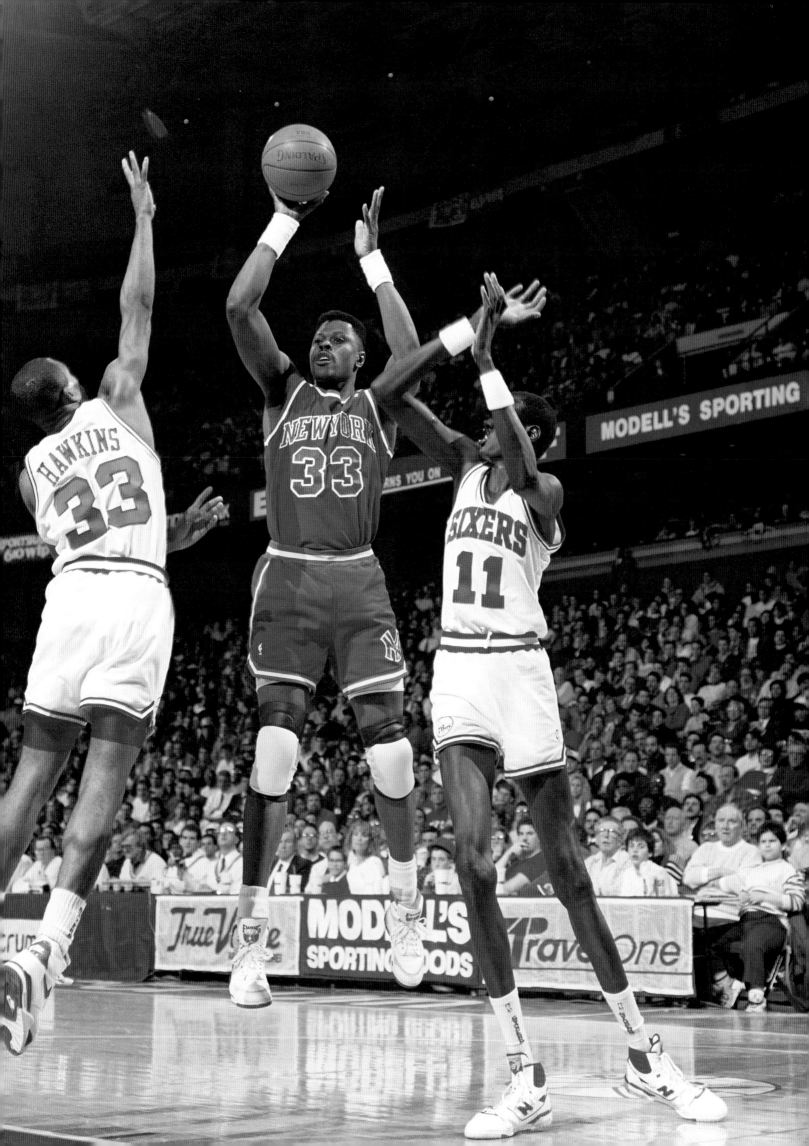

All this was expected from the beginning of his career because so coveted were his talents – and so worried were NBA officials about what clubs might do to get them – that they devised a "lottery pick" system in 1985 for teams not making the playoffs to determine their first-round selection position. The Knicks had the top pick that year, and they chose Ewing.

Though he was chosen the NBA's Rookie of the Year in 1986 and was the only rookie named to the All-Star team that year, he became a lightning rod for critics who had bought the idea that he was the "next" Bill Russell. Ewing, who had been tutored by Russell, had displayed some of those skills as a collegian. "He had an ability to coil and recoil on blocked shots, swatting one attempt away, and then recovering to go after another," said Dave Gavitt, former Boston Celtics GM. "We haven't seen that since Bill Russell."

So the comparisons were too easily tossed around when he entered the pros. Ewing responded in part by becoming the team's all-time blocked shot leader, and the first Knick ever to have two 2,000-point seasons. He also has led the Knicks in scoring every season.

Sometimes his game-controlling offense can be an awesome sight. For example, during one stretch of the 1992 season, he scored his team's final six points in the last 61 seconds of a game against Dallas, getting the game-winner with six seconds to play. Ten days later, against Detroit, he capped a 45-point performance with a fall-away jump shot with 20 seconds to play for the winning basket; and two days after that, he scored six straight points in the final two minutes to wipe out a four-point Charlotte lead in a Knicks' victory.

"I've never been out to copy anyone's style," says Ewing. "I just want to be known as one of the best ever."

Above left: *Patrick Ewing with All-Star rival Hakeem Olajuwon in 1988. Ewing led the Knicks to the 1994 NBA finals but lost to Olajuwon and the Rockets.*

Left: *Ewing ranks in the top 25 among the NBA's all-time playoff scorers, and is in the top five in blocked shots. He also is the Knicks' all-time playoff leader in games, points, blocks and rebounds.*

Opposite: *Opposing centers do not have the luxury of expecting Ewing always to post himself under the basket on offense, because he has added a good outside shot. When he moves to the outside they must go out and guard him, or allow him to create a mismatch against a smaller defender. If they do go out to face him, he then has more room for his strong inside moves that often ends with one of his patented dunks.*

HORACE GRANT

Position: Forward
College: Clemson
Drafted: Chicago, 1st Rd. ('87)

Birth Date: July 4, 1965
Height: 6' 10"
Weight: 220

In a move to surround center Shaquille O'Neal with more support under the basket and free him from constant double-teaming, Orlando signed forward Horace Grant as a free agent before the 1995 season after he had helped the Chicago Bulls win three straight NBA championships while playing with Michael Jordan. He then played a key role in helping the Magic into the NBA finals,

beating his old Bulls team including Jordan in the process, and he maintained his career average of nearly 13 points and nine rebounds a game.

Grant was a first round pick of the Bulls in 1987 and he teamed with Scottie Pippen, who had been chosen by Seattle on the 15th pick of that round, and Jordan to make the Bulls the most dominating NBA team of the early 1990s. A power forward, he was the team's top rebounder for his first four seasons and a second team All-NBA Defensive selection in his final two Chicago seasons.

Left: *The Chicago Bulls did not contend seriously for an NBA title until Horace Grant became power forward after being a first-round draft pick in 1987. He was Chicago's leading rebounder in six of his first seven seasons and became Orlando's major rebounding force after joining the Magic.*

Opposite: *Grant has made the NBA's All-Defensive second team three times but he also is a fine offensive player, having hit more than 50 percent of his shots every season. In 1996, he scored in double figures 51 times, and he amassed double figures 29 times in rebounds. Grant and Shaquille O'Neal together averaged 20 rebounds per game.*

Grant, whose twin brother Harvey also plays in the NBA, spurned richer offers than the $3 million he received to play for Orlando but he stressed that he wanted another chance to play for the championship. He also has assumed a leadership role with the younger Magic players.

"Horace has kept everybody from getting ahead of themselves," said teammate Brian Shaw. "He always wears one of his championship rings and something like that is all it takes to get everyone's attention."

Grant also brought to Orlando his unselfish style of play on the court, where he is content to bang the boards, play defense and add whatever points he can collect.

Those unique attributes were never unappreciated on the Chicago team. For example, in 1994, he led the Bulls in scoring ten times and the team won eight of those games.

Bulls coach Phil Jackson noted that Grant didn't get the notoriety that Jordan and Pippen received because he wasn't a featured offensive star. "We asked him to hit the boards, help our center, and allow the other two guys to do their thing, and he responded as well as we ever could have hoped," Jackson noted. The Bulls considered him on a par with the NBA's best power forwards. And the Chicago team has the championship rings to prove it.

TOM GUGLIOTTA

Position: Forward **Birth Date:** Dec. 19, 1969
College: N.C. State **Height:** 6' 10"
Drafted: Washington, 1st Rd. ('92) **Weight:** 240

Tom Gugliotta has been with three NBA teams in four seasons – the Washington Bullets, the Golden State Warriors and the Minnesota Timberwolves. But it is his current team, the Timberwolves, that is reaping the benefits of his considerable all-around talents.

In 1996, his first full season with the Wolves, he set records by averaging nine rebounds a game, and with his 28 double-doubles. He was the team's leading rebounder 42 times, its top scorer in 15 games and led the team in assists 11 times. Many underrate his athletic abilities but he was the number two dunker for the Wolves in 1996, with 67.

Gugliotta was a first round pick of the Washington Bullets in 1992, and their fans booed the selection. By the end of his first season, Gugliotta not only had won over many of the fans, but also became a first team selection on the NBA's all-rookie team.

Gugliotta, at 6' 10", is a big man who excels at passing and shooting. He also has shown a flair for shooting three-pointers, which opens up good passing lanes that allow him to take advantage of his fine ballhandling skills and his ability to create passing angles for himself. He has great court vision, and doesn't hesitate to get the ball to someone who might have a better shot than he does. He also plays defense and has played all three frontcourt positions, though he is best suited to the power forward spot.

"He's got skills and a physical presence," says coach Wes Unseld of the Bullets. "It's just a matter of how badly he wants it. But of everything I've seen of him, what I like is that he seems to want to try to be as good as he can be."

Tom was traded to the Golden State Warriors early in the 1995 season for 1994 Rookie of the Year Chris Webber; and later in the season, he was swapped for Donyell Marshall of Minnesota.

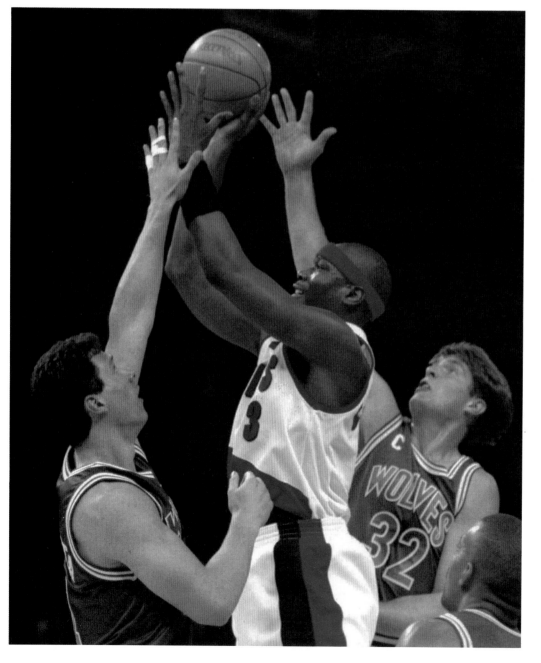

Left: *Tom Gugliotta played with the Washington Bullets and Golden State Warriors before being traded to Minnesota during the 1995 season. But with every team, he has shown remarkable all-around abilities in scoring, playmaking, rebounding and defense.*

Opposite left and right: *Anfernee Hardaway's great all-around skills, shooting, playmaking and rebounding earned him a starting job in the 1996 NBA All-Star Game. He has given the Orlando Magic more power in its backcourt with his 20 points per game average and his work as the team's top steal-maker.*

ANFERNEE HARDAWAY

Position: Guard   **Birth Date:** July 18, 1971
College: Memphis State   **Height:** 6' 7"
Drafted: Golden State, 1st Rd. ('93)   **Weight:** 195

Anfernee Hardaway has been pegged as a prototype 21st century player, because his incredible versatility renders conventional positions obsolete. One observer noted that the Orlando Magic, with Hardaway working together with center Shaquille O'Neal, "should be on exhibit at Orlando's famed EPCOT Center."

Hardaway is an almost perfect clone of Magic Johnson, the great Los Angeles Lakers' all-pro guard of the 1980s. Hardaway's athletic skills are such that he fits the same niche for his team that Johnson once did for his. Like Johnson, at 6' 7", he is big enough to be a small forward but is also effective as a point guard. Hardaway ran Orlando's offense during the second half of his rookie season, but because he is so skilled in all phases of the game, he sometimes appears to be restricted in the point guard's traditional job of passing first and shooting sec-

ond. When he is allowed to concentrate on scoring, he often does so with breathtaking slashes to the basket or by using his height advantage to shoot over smaller defenders. "He can get to the basket, he can shoot over smaller guards, he's a brilliant passer, and if he's fouled, he can knock down those shots, too," says his coach, Brian Hill, in an identical description to the role that Johnson played for the Lakers team.

Hardaway was just the player the Magic needed to push themselves into playoff status. He came to Orlando immediately after the Golden State Warriors made him their first draft pick in 1993, in a momentous trade that cost Orlando the rights to forward Chris Webber, who had been drafted by the Magic, and three Number 1 draft picks – quite a price to pay for a player who had never stepped on an NBA court.

But is was definitely worth it. Midway through his 1994 rookie season, Hardaway helped take control of the Magic's backcourt and provide all-pro center Shaquille O'Neal with a perfect set-up man and scorer. He was second to O'Neal in scoring, averaging more than 16 points per game in his rookie year and crashing the 20-point barrier in his second season.

Hardaway, an All-America at Memphis State who also was a unanimous choice on the 1994 NBA All-Rookie team, favors his nickname Penny. He earned first team status on the All-NBA team after the 1995 and 1996 seasons. In 1996, he was the only NBA player to score more than 20 points per game (21.7); have more than five assists (7.1); and shoot better than 50 percent (51.0).

Left: *Hardaway cost the Orlando Magic top draft pick Chris Webber and three No.1 draft picks. But general manager Pat Williams believed he was worth that steep price, and he proved to be right. In 1996, Hardaway won three games with last-second field goals.*

TIM HARDAWAY

Position: Guard **Birth Date:** Sept. 1, 1966
College: U Texas-El Paso **Height:** 6' 0"
Drafted: Golden State, 1st Rd. ('89) **Weight:** 170

Before Tim Hardaway even arrived in the NBA, he was downgraded as a pro prospect because of his size, lack of top competition and erratic shooting – except by former coach Don Nelson of Golden State. "Every time we saw him shoot, the ball went in," Nelson said. Many pundits wondered whether Tim Hardaway's NBA career was in jeopardy after a knee injury cost him the entire 1994 season. He answered them in his own way.

In 1995, he was named to the All-Star Game. He did it again in 1996 when he was en route to leading the Golden State Warriors in assists 37 times, and in scoring nine times. Later in the 1996 season, he was traded from the Golden State Warriors to the Miami Heat. He promptly set a Miami team and personal record with 19 assists in a game against the Milwaukee Bucks. In the playoffs, he also set a club record with 30 points against the Chicago Bulls, and during the season, he was eighth

Above: *Hardaway came to Miami from Golden State with Chris Gatling during the 1996 season in a trade for Kevin Willis and Bimbo Coles.*

Right: *In 1996, with Golden State and Miami, Hardaway finished eighth in the NBA in assists (8.0) and 15th in steals (1.65).*

in the NBA with an assists average of eight per game.

Even as a rookie, his crossover move to the hoop bamboozled the most experienced NBA guards. His weakness was shooting from the outside. So in his first off-season, he shot 300 to 500 balls every day, and since then he has offered two bad choices to opponents: Play him tight and be victimized by the quick crossover move to the basket, or play him loose to cut off that move and be nailed by the outside jumper.

He also has established himself as a brash, cocky trash-talker who backs down from no one. His scoring average went from 14.7 per game as a rookie to 22.9 and his first All-Star Game in his second season. He was there again in 1992, 1993,1995 and 1996.

"I expect to be in this game for many years to come," he said. "I have worked to be chosen as one of the best at my position in the NBA and I am just going to be me whenever I play."

The Miami Heat has developed a more physical, competitive style since Hardaway joined them. Point guard is a natural position for him with his instinctive, fiery leadership and adroit ballhandling.

Above: *Tim is a fiery competitor and received Golden State's McMahon Award as its most inspirational player when he was a rookie.*

Left: *Hardaway was a unanimous selection to the NBA's all-rookie team in 1990 after averaging 14.7 points per game. He has become a perennial selection to the All-Star team.*

Opposite: *With his physical playing style, his deft ballhandling skills and his crossover move to the hoop, Hardaway is one of the NBA's best point guards.*

HERSEY HAWKINS

Position: Guard
College: Bradley
Drafted: L.A. Clippers, 1st Rd. ('88)

Birth Date: Sept. 29, 1965
Height: 6' 3"
Weight: 190

It was no accident that after the Seattle Supersonics obtained Hersey Hawkins in a trade with the Charlotte Hornets they became NBA playoff contenders. Hawkins provided great stability in the Sonics backcourt and was a great counterbalance for the flamboyant Gary Payton, his playing partner.

The two form a deadly combination for opposing ball handlers. Payton finished first in steals in the NBA during the 1996 season with 231 and Hawkins was eighth with 149 – a total of 380 or nearly four a game. Hawkins was sixth in the NBA in foul shooting during the 1996 season with a .873 percentage; and he was among the NBA's best three-point shooters.

In stints with both Philadelphia and Charlotte before coming to Seattle, Hawkins showed that he possessed the tools to become a fine NBA backcourt player. The early part of his career in Philadelphia was played in the huge shadow of Charles Barkley. Although he did make his mark by being named to the NBA's all-rookie first team. He also scored 1,196 points, the most ever by a Philadelphia rookie. But when Barkley was traded to Phoenix for the 1993 season, Hawkins enlarged his own niche as a playmaker and three-point shooter par excellence.

Hawkins was an All-America player at Bradley University, where he was a near-unanimous selection as Player of the Year in 1988. He was also the nation's leading collegiate scorer that year.

Right: Hersey Hawkins was the perfect backcourt partner for Gary Payton in Seattle, where their ballhandling accounted for 380 steals during the Supersonics' run for the 1996 NBA Western Conference title.

GRANT HILL

Position: Forward **Birth Date:** Oct. 5, 1972
College: Duke **Height:** 6' 8"
Drafted: Detroit, 1st Rd. ('94) **Weight:** 225

How good is Grant Hill? In 1995, he was the first NBA rookie to lead the All-Star voting, drawing more than one million votes, and surpassing such tried-and-true all-stars as David Robinson, Shaquille O'Neal, Hakeem Olajuwon and Charles Barkley. He did it again in 1996. Hill is so talented that even before his rookie season had ended, he was a unanimous choice to hit the same star status as such NBA icons as Michael Jordan, Larry Bird and Magic Johnson.

Hill is the son of former NFL star Calvin Hill, and has his dad's trademark pedigree of talent and class. A slashing, above-the-rim player, Hill has already created as much excitement in the NBA as he did during his All-America years at Duke when he helped the Blue Devils win back-to-back NCAA titles.

Unlike many highly touted rookies who hold out for big money and hurt the start of their careers, Hill signed immediately for a tidy $44 million and he has more than fulfilled all expectations. In 1996 he became the first NBA player ever to lead a team in points (1,618), rebounds (783) and assists (548) in the same season. During that season he also led the NBA in triple-doubles with ten, and he was ranked among the top 20 players in four different categories while getting most of the defensive attention from Pistons' opponents.

Above: *Grant Hill moved right into the Detroit Pistons' starting lineup as a rookie and not only averaged 20 points per game, but also led the team in scoring during most of his first season. He was the only rookie to make the 1995 NBA All-Star team.*

Right: *Hill, who is a fan favorite in every NBA city because of his classy attitude and fiery play, was named to Dream Team III, the 1996 U.S. Olympic basketball team.*

TYRONE HILL

Position: Forward
College: Xavier
Drafted: Golden State, 1st Rd. ('90)

Birth Date: Mar. 17, 1968
Height: 6' 9"
Weight: 245

Tyrone Hill is a perfect example of a "late bloomer." He was a first round pick of the Golden State Warriors in 1990 and then played without much distinction for three seasons with Golden State and one with the Cavaliers, to whom he was traded for a Number 1 draft pick before the 1994 season. He never averaged even 10 points during those seasons, but he did show good rebounding strength, particularly in 1993, when he averaged 10 per game for the Warriors.

In his second season with the Cavs, Hill took off, stepping in to provide both the rebounding and the scoring the team sorely needed when center Brad Daugherty went out for the 1995 season with injuries. Hill became a league leader in both categories, but he was still more content to work on improving his game rather than taking advantage of his newly-acquired status. He disdained a spot on the 1995 NBA All-Star ballot in favor of veteran teammates Mark Price and Hot Rod Williams, but was later named to the All-Star team anyway. In 1996, he was injured in a car accident and missed nearly half the season, but returned for the playoffs.

As a youngster, Hill tried to pattern his game after former Los Angeles Lakers great James Worthy. "I wanted to do everything just like him, drive to the basket the way he did."

One of Hill's greatest attributes is knowing his limitations and working within them. He is not a leaper or a ball handler, but he is relentless under the basket. In one game against Miami, he grabbed 10 rebounds in one quarter. "He's like a silent storm trooper," said his coach, Mike Fratello. "He comes in, goes after every ball relentlessly, then goes home."

Left: *Tyrone Hill got the opportunity to shine for the Cleveland Cavaliers when center Brad Daugherty was injured and many of his front court responsibilities fell to Hill, who had been only a journeyman during three previous seasons with the Golden State Warriors*

JEFF HORNACEK

Position: Guard
College: Iowa State
Drafted: Phoenix, 2nd Rd. ('86)

Birth Date: May 3, 1963
Height: 6' 4"
Weight: 190

Jeff Hornacek makes the "fine wine" team.

He just keeps getting better with age, as the Utah Jazz have discovered since obtaining him from the Philadelphia 76ers for guard Jeff Malone in 1994. He helped the Jazz to the Western Conference Finals in 1996 and helps to form a great backcourt for Utah by teaming with another All-Star guard, John Stockton.

Hornacek was part of the Phoenix Suns Dynamic Duo backcourt combination with Kevin Johnson for many years before being traded to the Philadelphia 76ers in 1992 for Charles Barkley.

With Philadelphia, he kept close to his 20-point scoring average with a 19-point mark on a team not nearly as talented as Phoenix.

Hornacek still is among Phoenix's top five in all-time free throws, shooting, assists and steals; in addition, he finished first in each of those categories in at least one season.

Above: *Jeff Hornacek is renowned for his playmaking, beginning with his rookie season with Phoenix when he set team records of 13 assists in a half, and 10 in a quarter. During his college years at Iowa State, Hornacek was only the second Big Eight player ever to accumulate more than 1,000 points and 600 assists; and his 665 total assists were a Big Eight career record.*

Left: *Jeff Hornacek, who had set records in both Phoenix and Philadelphia before being traded to the Utah Jazz for Jeff Malone, was a perfect fit in the Jazz backcourt with John Stockton, since both are superb playmakers. Between them, they average 30 points and 15 assists per game.*

JIM JACKSON

Position: Guard   **Birth Date:** Oct. 14, 1970
College: Ohio State   **Height:** 6' 6"
Drafted: Dallas, 1st Rd. ('92)   **Weight:** 220

Jim Jackson survived an unusual rookie NBA season in 1993, during which he played only 28 games because of a contract dispute, to become one of the Dallas Mavericks' best players. He averaged 16 points in that limited rookie action, then pumped it up to 18 points despite another woeful season by his team in 1994.

But under new coach Dick Motta and teaming with Jamal Mashburn, he has begun to amass the points and performances long anticipated after his All-America seasons at Ohio State University. During the 1995 season, he and Mashburn became only the sixth pair of teammates ever to score 50 points in separate games during one season.

From the start, Jackson has contributed some clutch shooting as well as good on-the-floor direction. "Jim has the ability to make the players around him reach deep into their games," Mavs general manager Rick Sund noted. In his first NBA game, having practiced just one time, he had four assists.

On a five-game road trip late that season, during which the Mavericks won three games, he averaged 19 points, nearly six rebounds and seven assists; and he had a 27-point, eight-rebound, seven-assist game against the Washington Bullets.

Jackson, who gave up his senior year at Ohio State to turn pro, has impressed many in the NBA.

"I think he will be a superstar in this league," said Sacramento general manager Jerry Reynolds. Phoenix guard Kevin Johnson called him "the real deal," and former Denver coach Dan Issel particularly liked his air of cockiness that lends a special aura to the league's best players.

Quinn Buckner, his coach during the 1994 season, said that Jackson's toughness and ability to make those around him look better will ultimately make him a star in the same mold as Kevin Johnson.

Right: *One former teammate said of Jim Jackson, "If he gets his shooting down, he could be another Michael Jordan because he can do whatever he wants on the court to get his shot and he is so strong that if you put a body on him, he just shrugs it off." That's what happened in 1996 when he was among the NBA's top 25 scorers.*

KEVIN JOHNSON

Position: Guard
College: U Cal-Berkeley
Drafted: Cleveland, 1st Rd. ('87)

Birth Date: Mar. 6, 1966
Height: 6' 1"
Weight: 190

Kevin Johnson has been selected to the All-NBA team several times, made appearances in the All-Star Game, helped his team to the Western Conference championships in 1993, and is considered one of the NBA's best all-around guards.

He has played in the NBA for nine season and shows no signs of slackening the tremendous energy that he pours into the game. He became the 23rd player in NBA history, sixth among those active in 1996, to score 11,000 points and accumulate 5,000 assists. Always one of the NBA's great playmakers, he averaged 9.2 assists, sixth in the league, and was tops on the Suns for the sixth time in seven seasons. He had 10 or more assists in 23 games, and handed out 14 or more nine times, including a season-high 19 against Dallas late in the season.

Kevin has always been a slashing driver to the basket and a fine jump shooter. In 1996, he was the Suns' number two scorer with 18.7 points per game, scoring more than 20 points in 23 games and topping 30 points four times.

In short, no one in the NBA has a better all-around game, and part of the credit for that goes to his coach Cotton Fitzsimmons, who during his first tour as coach

Above: *Kevin Johnson cost the Suns a bundle when they obtained him from the Cleveland Cavaliers, but he has been a perennial member of the NBA's post-season all-star teams.*

Left: *Johnson has often led the club in scoring and assists, and he is at his best when he takes his offense directly at the opposition.*

Page 42: *Johnson is an excellent all-around player known for his unselfish game.*

Page 43: *In 1996, Kevin Johnson became the 23rd player in NBA history to tally 11,000 points and 5,000 rebounds.*

of the Suns, chided Johnson for being too unselfish with the ball by distributing it to his teammates and passing up too many open shots.

Fitzsimmons even commended Johnson for getting everyone involved in his playmaking. "But," he added, "you are not taking your jump shot enough and we are not scoring enough points to win. I want you to be a shooter first, a playmaker second."

Johnson came to the Suns in a monster trade with the Cleveland Cavaliers. The Cavs dismissed the potential of Johnson, though he was a number one pick that season. He left the University of California at Berkeley as the school's all-time scorer, assist-maker and leader in steals.

While Kevin can make slashing drives to the basket, he also has a good outside shot. His coaches want him to utilize it more rather than incurring all of the physical pounding that his drives inflict. Yet, as he showed in the 1993 NBA playoffs, he is an adroit penetrator. He also has great stamina – he was the only Suns player to play all but one minute of the historic triple-overtime win against Chicago in the playoffs. Since 1993, he has missed just 14 games due to injury following the All-Star break.

LARRY JOHNSON

Position: Forward
College: UNLV
Drafted: Charlotte, 1st Rd. ('91)

Birth Date: Mar. 14, 1969
Height: 6' 6"
Weight: 250

Larry Johnson brought himself a lot of attention during his early NBA seasons with his distinctive gold tooth, his hilarious TV commercial as a "rammin'-jammin' grandmama" and his on-court performances that even outdid all of the experts' career predictions.

Johnson, the star of UNLV's 1990 national championship team and a two-time first team All-America, was the first player picked in the 1991 NBA draft. He signed a six-year contract for nearly $20 million, though some NBA people said he was too small at 6' 6" to play power forward in the NBA.

Tell it to the teams who faced him, beginning with the New Jersey Nets who, after Johnson had been a member of the Hornets for just three days, watched him pull down 18 rebounds against them.

Since coming into the NBA, Johnson has battled back from a serious back injury that almost jeopardized his career. He always has averaged around 20 points per game and has consistently led his team in scoring and rebound-

ing. In his rookie season, he averaged 19.1 shots and 11 rebounds per game. He was named to the NBA's second team All-Pro list after his second season in 1993.

He is incredibly strong for his size, and one NFL scout declared he would make it in pro football. His long arms help him play as "big" as power forwards who are four and five inches taller. Even before his rookie season had ended, he was being compared with such all-stars as Charles Barkley and Karl Malone for his great determination to grab rebounds. He is Charlotte's all-time leading rebounder. Johnson signed with the New York Knicks after the 1996 season.

Boston's Larry Bird, after just two head-to-head confrontations, noted: "He's strong, quick and very aggressive. He is powerful and when he goes after the ball, he can jump over anybody."

He's our building block, our foundation, our untouchable," said former Hornets coach Allan Bristow.

Below left: *Larry Johnson has averaged nearly 20 points per game and is Charlotte's all-time leading rebounder.*

Below: *Johnson, the NBA's No.1 draft pick in 1991, was chosen its Rookie of the Year in 1992.*

Left: *Larry Johnson wears jersey No. 2 in honor of Jerry Tarkanian, his coach at UNLV where both of them enjoyed the 1990 NCAA championship.*

Below left: *Johnson also laid waste to predictions that at 6' 6", he couldn't play forward in the NBA: He has scored over 6,000 points and grabbed more than 3,000 rebounds.*

Below: *Johnson and teammate Glen Rice have become one of the NBA's most powerful scoring duos. In 1996, they were ranked fourth in scoring.*

Page 46: *Johnson's great strength and drive make him a problem for NBA defenders.*

MICHAEL JORDAN

Left: *Michael Jordan is a master of NBA levitation, with an endless repertoire of shots that seem to take him eye level with the basket.*

Below: *Jordan still is the nation's most recognizable athlete, both from his playing and from his steady stream of endorsements.*

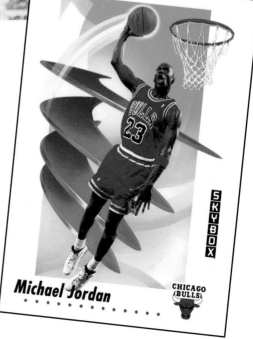

Michael Jordan

SKYBOX

CHICAGO BULLS

Position: Guard   **Birth Date:** Feb. 17, 1963
College: North Carolina   **Height:** 6' 6"
Drafted: Chicago, 1st Rd. ('84)   **Weight:** 198

Michael.

That's all you need to say, and everyone knows the subject is Michael Jordan. It is like that the world over, because Jordan is unquestionably the best-known athlete in the universe, particularly after he led the Chicago Bulls to their fourth NBA title in six years in 1996.

Jordan's story is as remarkable as his talents. He left the Chicago Bulls after leading them to their third straight NBA title in 1993 to try his hand at professional baseball. But after a year and a half, he so missed basketball that he returned to the Bulls late in the 1995 season and helped Chicago get into the NBA playoffs. He was not exactly the Jordan of old – although most other players would have been considered all-stars had they played as well – and the Bulls were eliminated by the Orlando

Magic in the second round of the Eastern Conference championships. Jordan resolved to work harder than ever to regain his basketball skills, and a year later, Chicago set an NBA record with 72 regular season victories and went on to win the finals against the Sonics, and Jordan won his fourth NBA Most Valuable Player Award, the MVP award in the playoffs and his eighth scoring title.

He also was invited to become a member of Dream Team III, the 1996 U.S. Olympic basketball team, but he declined the opportunity to earn an unprecedented third Olympic basketball gold medal, saying: "I've had my medals. Give someone else a chance to earn one."

Jordan has rewritten the record book. He and Wilt Chamberlain are the only players ever to score 3,000 points in one season, and in 1993, he broke Chamberlain's record of six straight NBA scoring titles when he won his seventh while leading the Bulls to their third straight NBA championship – only the third team ever to accomplish that feat.

A spontaneous player, Jordan has said: "I don't plan all that stuff. It just happens." But it happens because of his marvelous athletic ability that allows him to change direction and shoot while hanging in the air.

While his lifetime offensive numbers are dynamic, he gets more personal satisfaction from his work on defense, underscored by his perennial standing on the NBA's All-Defensive team. His speed and ability to anticipate helped him to become the first player ever to record 200 steals in one season.

Top right: *Michael Jordan and Charles Barkley waged a two-man war in the 1993 NBA Finals and in the end, Jordan's heroic play during the last minutes of the sixth game proved to be decisive.*

Right: *Jordan exults with Dream Team mate Scottie Pippen (left) after helping the U.S. basketball team to a gold medal in the 1992 Olympics.*

Opposite: *Michael Jordan has played on NCAA, Olympic and NBA title teams. Before he won four NBA titles, his game-winning basket in the final seconds helped North Carolina win the NCAA title in his freshman year; and two years after that, he was on America's gold medal team in the 1984 Olympics. He earned a second gold medal on the 1992 Olympic team.*

Page 50: *Because of his ability to shoot while leaping over and around defenders and his own excellent defensive skills, Jordan is considered the greatest player in NBA history.*

SHAWN KEMP

Left: *Shawn Kemp is renowned for his great leaping ability. He won rebounding titles at Seattle in five of his first six seasons. During one of his appearances in Magic Johnson's All-Star Game, he scored 49 points with a variety of high-flying dunks. He was just as spectacular in Larry Bird's All-Star invitational game in his native Indiana. As a 19-year-old rookie, he led the NBA Slam Dunk Competition for the first two rounds and finished fourth.*

Position: Forward
College: None
Drafted: Seattle, 1st Rd. ('89)

Birth Date: Nov. 26, 1969
Height: 6' 10"
Weight: 245

Shawn Kemp placed himself firmly among the elite of the NBA during the 1996 playoffs with an outstanding performance for the Seattle Supersonics against the Chicago Bulls. He led the Sonics in scoring and was a mighty force around the basket, a carry-over from his regular season performance when he was an All-NBA second team selection for the third year in a row.

Kemp led his team in four categories while helping it to the Western Conference championship: scoring, with 1,550 points and a 19.6 average (No. 22 in the NBA); rebounding, with 904 for an 11.4 average (No. 5 in the NBA); field goal percentage, with .561 (also No. 5 in

the league); and in blocked shots, with 127 (No. 17 in the NBA).

Kemp is also a rarity in NBA history in that he was drafted without having played college basketball. But lack of college experience has not proven to be a detriment. Kemp was named to start in the 1994, 1995 and 1996 All-Star games for the Western Conference.

Kemp was also the first back-to-back All-Star Game performer from the Sonics since Jack Sikma in the mid-1980s.

He also was a member of the U.S. gold medal-winning Dream Team II at the World Basketball Championships in 1994, starting five of the eight games, including the medal-deciding contest against Russia.

"The things he always had going for him along with his natural skills to rebound and block shots, were his

Above: *Seattle's Shawn Kemp battles Denver's Rodney Rogers. Kemp has become the Supersonics' big force with his scoring, rebounding and all-around defense.*

Left: *Kemp didn't have the luxury of developing his skills in college and had to learn the game in the cauldron of NBA competition. His ability to survive and to perfect his game is a tribute to his skills.*

love for the game and his work ethic," says his former coach, K.C. Jones. "You can't teach those things. He didn't have any college experience as a base so he worked on the fundamental parts of the game – when to shoot, when to drive, learning to take what's there."

Patience was his biggest virtue. He started just one of his 81 games as a rookie and became the starting power forward in the 16th game of his second season. That year he led his team in scoring 13 times, in rebounding 35 times, and was the best shot-blocker.

"When I was first drafted, I wanted everything," Kemp said. "Then I got a feel for what this game is all about – the people who can help you, the people who can hurt you, how to prepare every night for a game. That became my job and my life."

Kemp finally received some recognition in 1993 when

Left: *Shawn Kemp is a rarity in NBA history – one of just a very few players to come directly into the NBA with no major college experience. In 1988-89, he was enrolled first at the University of Kentucky and then at Trinity Valley Community College in Texas but never played for either school before entering the 1989 draft.*

Page 54: *Kemp has increased both his scoring and rebounding averages each season and has made several All-Star Game appearances, indicating his talent as a great all-around player.*

he was picked for the NBA All-Star Game for the first time, and then led the Sonics into the Western Conference playoff finals.

He was also Seattle's number one rebounder and shot-blocker, and was third in steals.

But the strength of his game is under the basket. When he seemed to stray from it after hobnobbing with his All-Star teammates, his coach George Karl ordered a halt to his fancy approach, and he responded with a fine second-half season performance, and has maintained a steady performance ever since.

"Shawn's pro career is just beginning to blossom," Karl said. "He can become one of the NBA's fine players if he just continues to play as hard, learn and improve. Most of all he must do what he does best, and that is work the boards."

TONI KUKOC

Left: *Toni Kukoc had to upgrade his game from European competition to that of the NBA, with the added burden of trying to fill the gap in the Bulls' lineup left by the retirement of Michael Jordan. When Jordan returned in 1995, he told Kukoc to relax and play his natural style, and the two meshed well.*

Position: Forward
College: None
Drafted: Chicago, 2nd Rd. ('90)

Birth Date: Sept. 18, 1968
Height: 6' 11"
Weight: 230

Toni Kukoc was a two-time Olympian and considered the most talented player in Europe when he finally joined the Chicago Bulls for the 1994 season. He played on Yugoslavia's silver medal-winning team in the 1988 Olympics and for the Croatian silver medalists in 1992. In between those stints, he was the Bulls' second round draft pick in 1990. The Bulls then waited patiently for him to finish his European commitments before coming to the NBA.

When Kukoc arrived in Chicago he was seen as the immediate replacement for Michael Jordan, who had retired after the 1993 season to play baseball. Kukoc was deeply disappointed in not getting an opportunity to play with Jordan – the main reason he signed with the Bulls late in 1994 – and was likewise elated when Jordan returned late in 1994.

Kukoc has overcome many cultural differences in adapting himself to life in the NBA, including the need to upgrade his game to the NBA levels. He has become a valuable swing man for the Bulls, spelling both Jordan and Pippen, and providing Chicago with instant offense whenever he comes into a game. Kukoc can play both forward and guard, and he also is a 40 percent three-point shooter.

CHRISTIAN LAETTNER

Position: Forward
College: Duke
Drafted: Minnesota, 1st Rd. ('92)

Birth Date: Aug. 17, 1969
Height: 6' 11"
Weight: 235

"Christian Laettner", said one of his ex-Timberwolves teammates, "is the straw that stirs the drink."

As a collegian, Laettner helped Duke to back-to-back NCAA championships and four consecutive appearances in the Final Four. His last-second, game-winning shot against Kentucky in the 1992 Final Four semifinals will always be remembered as one of the greatest clutch plays in college basketball history. That year, he was chosen college basketball's Player of the Year.

Laettner was the only college player on the 1992 U.S. Olympic gold medal Dream Team, and then hit the NBA trail with a bang that startled many who did not realize that, on the court, he has always been a "baby-faced assassin." His boyish good looks mask a toughness and tenacity that have made him a fierce all-around competitor. In the NBA he immediately went toe-to-toe with the league's rebounding heavyweights and set many club rebounding records, gaining respect for his willingness to do this "grunt" work. He has kept a credible 17 points-per-game scoring average.

Laettner, who often clashed with teammates, opponents and officials in fits of frustration over the Wolves' non-achievement, was traded to Atlanta during the 1996 season. With the Hawks he no longer must carry the scoring and rebounding load, and should better display his great skills.

DAN MAJERLE

Position: Guard/Forward   **Birth Date:** Sept. 9, 1965
College: Central Michigan   **Height:** 6' 6"
Drafted: Phoenix, 1st Rd. ('88)   **Weight:** 220

The toughness that Dan Majerle (pronounced MAR-LEE) exhibited during the 1988 Olympics has helped him throughout his NBA career. The Phoenix Suns admired his "blue collar" skills so much that they drafted him even before he was elected to the U.S. Olympic team. Majerle had come from Central Michigan University, and had won a spot on the team against players from more glamorous college basketball backgrounds.

In Phoenix, and now in Cleveland, Majerle has become renowned for his valuable role as "sixth man" and for his hard-nosed defensive ability. He usually faces the opposition's top scorer but he also carries a great offensive weapon with his three-point shooting skill. He set a league record with 192 three-pointers in 1994 and led the Cavs in 1996. Majerle also is third on the NBA playoff list with 347 three-pointers.

Dan can play both forward and guard, and he has been a member of the NBA's All-Defensive teams.

Left: *Dan Majerle gained notoriety for his tough defense for the U.S. during the 1988 Olympics, in which his team won a bronze medal. His hard-nosed defense carried over to the NBA, as a first-round pick of the Phoenix Suns in 1988, after starring at Central Michigan University. He was traded to the Cleveland Cavaliers before the 1996 season.*

Opposite: *Christian Laettner was the only non-NBA member of the gold medal 1992 U.S. Olympic team. He used that experience of playing with the NBA's greatest players before joining the Minnesota Timberwolves as their first-round pick – third overall in the 1992 draft – to mark himself as a future star.*

KARL MALONE

Position: Forward **Birth Date:** July 24, 1963
College: Louisiana Tech **Height:** 6' 9"
Drafted: Utah, 1st Rd. ('85) **Weight:** 256

"The Mailman – because he delivers." A sportswriter in Louisiana hung that moniker on Karl Malone when he played for Louisiana Tech in the early eighties, and it belongs to him forever.

A marvelously sculpted power forward for the Utah Jazz, Malone has toiled long and hard during off-seasons on the weight equipment in the basement of his Salt Lake City home. He has been selected to the All-NBA team in eight consecutive seasons (1989-96), and is a regular participant in the NBA's All-Star Game, where he was picked as MVP in 1989 and co-MVP in 1993.

Malone has worked hard to raise the level of his game to the point where he has no peers as a power forward. "In this business, everyone always says what you can't do," Malone said. "Guys say you can't shoot outside so you start shooting from the outside and making them. Then it's that you can't play defense so you start playing defense. You throw it back at those critics."

Case in point: As a rookie, Malone's foul shooting accuracy was a miserable 49 percent. He now is a consistent 70 percent shooter.

"He is 100 percent better than when he started," says Jazz coach Jerry Sloan. "You know some guys go out the same way they come in. Not Karl. He has always done the things he needed to become better and now he's be-

Opposite: *Karl Malone, who played at Louisiana Tech, is one of the NBA's best power forwards. He is always among the league's top producers in games played, points, and rebounds. Karl has scored more than 2,000 points for nine consecutive seasons, and more than 23,000 in his career.*

Right: *Malone brushes aside complaints by opponents that he is too rough around the basket and stuffs home one of his patented jams. He's done that in 385 consecutive games through the 1996 season — and he has scored in double figures in each of those games.*

come one of the NBA's best post-up players."

Utah president Frank Layden, who was Malone's first coach with the Jazz, has two distinct images of Malone. Around the basket, he says, Karl reminds him of a heavyweight boxing champion by the way he utilizes his strength and moves. Layden also compares him to Jim Brown, the great NFL Hall of Fame running back. "Karl has the same kind of physical strength, quickness, good hands and mental toughness," Layden says. "The big thing about Karl is that he can catch the ball. He'll catch anything that's thrown to him, and then he lets his other skills take over."

Malone has averaged more than 25 points a game during his career. He also pulls down an average of 12 rebounds a game.

One of his chief assets is playing with all-pro guard John Stockton. Ironically, Malone and Stockton knew each other even before they became teammates at Utah because both were cut by coach Bobby Knight from the 1984 U.S. Olympic gold medal team. In 1992 and 1996, both were unanimous choices for America's Olympic basketball team.

The two have established such an amazing rapport together that they often are referred to as "Stockalone." Malone utilizes Stockton's excellent ability to get him the ball on the fast break; and Stockton thrives on Malone's fine talent of catching a pass in traffic and finishing a play.

"I'm very happy to play with him all these years," Stockton says. "He's made my job easier."

JAMAL MASHBURN

Position: Forward   **Birth Date:** Nov. 29, 1972
College: Kentucky   **Height:** 6' 8"
Drafted: Dallas, 1st Rd. ('93)   **Weight:** 240

Jamal Mashburn moved quite naturally from the All-America first team during his collegiate career at Kentucky to the NBA's All-Rookie first team after his first season with the Dallas Mavericks.

Mashburn brought tremendous scoring credentials into the NBA. He led all rookies with his 19.2 point scoring average in his first season, and he became the first Maverick to surpass 1,000 points since Sam Perkins in 1989. But most of all, he impressed everyone in the NBA with his continued intensity, despite the fact that the Mavs won only 13 times – the worst record in the 1994 NBA season. Still, Mashburn led his team in scoring 37 times; was first in rebounds 13 times; and led the team in assists 16 times. He hit double figures in scoring in 73 of his 79 games, including 37 20-point games and 7 in which he scored 30 or more points.

Left: *Jamal Mashburn brought great intensity to the Dallas Mavericks as their No. 1 draft pick in 1993, and turned it into All-Rookie honors as he became the first Dallas player in five years to score more than 1,000 points in his first season.*

Opposite: *Mashburn was the perfect complement to two other young Dallas players – Jim Jackson and Jason Kidd, also No. 1 picks. They promised to lead the lowly Mavs back to contender status during the last half of the 1990s.*

"Everyone knew he had the skills, but he also proved that he had the mental toughness to blot out the problems around him and play up to his capabilities," one NBA coach noted. "You just wonder what will happen when everything is going well for his team and he's playing in a relaxed almosphere. It may not be a pretty sight for the rest of the NBA."

Dallas coach Dick Motta, who took over in Mashburn's second season, revamped his forward-oriented offense specifically to give Mashburn more shots, and Mashburn has since become one of the NBA's fine young forwards. But before that season began, Motta had to enlist the aid of two former players, Mark Aguirre and Rolando Blackmon, to convince Mashburn that Motta's offense would take advantage of his shooting skills. "You'll get so many shots, your arm will fall off," Aguirre told him.

His prediction came true when Mashburn averaged more than 20 points per game while teaming with Jim Jackson, giving the Mavericks a solid 1-2 offensive punch. During the 1995 season, Mashburn and Jackson each turned in separate 50-point scoring feats – only the sixth time in NBA history that teammates have achieved that milestone in the same season. Mashburn delivered his in an overtime victory against Chicago. Earlier in Mashburn's rookie season, he and Jackson had combined to score more than 50 points nine times, and they once compiled 60 points against Orlando.

Mashburn was en route to another fine season in 1996, averaging more than 23 points per game when knee surgery sidelined him for the year after he played just 18 games. He is expected to make a full recovery and resume his all-star career.

Former NBA coach Chuck Daly noted: "He reminds me of Larry Bird. He's a passer who has a post-up game and an outside game. He has a chance to be a premier player in the game."

REGGIE MILLER

Position: Guard **Birth Date:** Aug. 24, 1965
College: UCLA **Height:** 6' 7"
Drafted: Indiana, 1st Rd. ('87) **Weight:** 185

There is no finer three-point field goal shooter in the NBA than Reggie Miller. And no one has quicker hands – or a faster mouth.

Miller is the Indiana Pacers' all-time leading scorer in both the regular and the post-season. During the 1996 season, he became the second NBA player ever to amass more than 1,200 career three-pointers. He has scored 100 or more three-point field goals for seven seasons in a row (1990-96). He put on one of the greatest scoring shows in NBA playoff history in 1994 when he knocked down a record-tying five three-pointers among the record-setting 25 points he scored in the fourth quarter of the Eastern Conference finals against the New York Knicks. He had a career high 39 playoff points in that game.

Miller, a guard, also accumulated more than 100 steals in five consecutive seasons. He consistently ranks among the NBA's top free throw shooters, and he is the NBA's premier trash-talker, marked by his game-long, vibrant

Above: *Reggie Miller is one of the NBA's best three-point shooters and holds the Pacers' all-time record. In the 1993 season, he made 163 three-pointers and once had a streak in which he hit one or more of those shots in 108 straight games.*

Right: *In addition to Miller's exploits at UCLA and in the NBA, his sister Cheryl was inducted into the Hall of Fame in 1995 after an All-America career at Southern Cal.*

Opposite: *When Reggie Miller finished his career at UCLA, he was second in all-time scoring to Kareem Abdul-Jabbar. He made the transition from high-scoring college forward to a solid NBA backcourt player, and added a good defensive touch with several seasons of more than 100 steals.*

exchanges with filmmaker Spike Lee, who was sitting at courtside during the Pacers-Knicks playoff series in 1994 and 1995.

Miller was a member of the 1996 U.S. Olympic Dream Team III after being a tri-captain of the U.S. Dream Team II that won the World Basketball Championships in 1994. He was also that team's No. 2 scorer, including a tourney-leading 30 three-pointers.

Miller comes from a family in which athletic excellence is the norm. His sister, Cheryl, is a Hall of Fame basketball player; and his brother, Darrell, was a major league catcher for five years with the California Angels.

It hardly seemed possible that Reggie would ever match his siblings' athletic achievements. For the first four years of his life, he slept with steel braces on his legs after having been born with pronated hips. Doctors said he might never walk normally.

But Reggie had to compete to survive in his family, and though overmatched for many years in the furious basketball games played in the Miller driveway, he developed his own game. He became a strong, talented player who was an All-America at UCLA and finished second on the school's all-time scoring list behind Lew Alcindor (Kareem Abdul-Jabbar).

ALONZO MOURNING

Position: Center   **Birth Date:** Feb. 8, 1970
College: Georgetown   **Height:** 6' 10"
Drafted: Charlotte, 1st Rd. ('92)   **Weight:** 240

Alonzo Mourning so impressed NBA observers during his rookie season in 1993 that the consensus was that he would be at least the equal of Shaquille O'Neal, the league's other great rookie center that season, when the

two finally grew up and became NBA veterans.

One observer noted that Mourning was "a throwback to the days when men were men and centers were centers, and not namby-pamby turnaround jump shooters." He plays with a healthy meanness that concedes nothing at either end of the floor, and he has become a physically and emotionally intimidating force.

"I think down there is what separates the men from

Left: *Alonzo Mourning was just what Miami needed to make the playoffs in 1996. During his NBA career with Charlotte and the Miami Heat, he quickly proved to be more than just a defensive force despite predictions when the Hornets made him the second pick of the 1992 draft. He followed in the tradition of great centers at Georgetown that also produced Patrick Ewing of the N.Y. Knicks and Dikembe Mutombo of the Denver Nuggets.*

Opposite: *Alonzo Mourning's impact on the Miami Heat was immediate following his trade from the Charlotte Hornets. He helped the team make the playoffs while leading the Heat in five statistical departments. He also finished among the NBA's top ten in 1996 in both scoring and rebounding, and he was one of four players to score more than 50 points in a game that season.*

the boys," he said. "Not too many people want to play down there, to take those elbows, the pushing and scratching. But I like that. I thrive on that. You can overpower people down there."

And he often does, in a raw, often volatile manner that earned him 15 technical fouls as a rookie. As a rebounder, he goes after everything on the glass.

After playing in a highly disciplined system at Georgetown for four years, Alonzo came out firing in the NBA. He doesn't hesitate to shoot the ball from any place within 20 feet of the basket, and finished his rookie year with a very respectable 21-point average.

Mourning was traded to the Miami Heat for all-star forward Glen Rice just as the 1996 season began and his impact was electric in both his team and individual play. He nearly rewrote the Heat's record book in just one year

and helped his team to the playoffs.

Alonzo became the first Miami player – and one of just six NBA players during that season – to average more than 20 points and 10 rebounds a game. He finished as the league's No. 7 scorer with 23.2 points per game, and its No. 8 rebounder with 10.4. Mourning also set a team and personal high with nine blocked shots and seven rebounds in a game against the Celtics; and he set another team mark with 22 rebounds against his old Hornets team. His 50 points against Atlanta made him just one of only four NBA players to score that many points in a 1996 game and it established a personal career mark.

In his second appearance in the playoffs (he had led Charlotte to post-season play in 1993), he led the Heat in scoring and matched another Heat newcomer, Tim Hardaway, with a team single-game scoring record of 30 against the Chicago Bulls.

Mourning also was a member of Dream Team II, the U.S. all-star team that won the World Basketball Championships in 1994.

Opposite: *In the NBA, Alonzo Mourning has worn jersey number 33, the same number worn by Patrick Ewing, his off-season tutor during Alonzo's years with the Hoyas.*

Right: *After the Charlotte Hornets picked Alonzo Mourning as the second player in the 1992 NBA draft, an immediate rivalry was created between him and Shaquille O'Neal, the top draft pick that year of the Orlando Magic, as to who would become the NBA's new dominant young center. Mourning is right there with O'Neal and his battles with other great centers like David Robinson and fellow Georgetown alumni Patrick Ewing and Dikembe Mutombo have highlighted his great talents.*

DIKEMBE MUTOMBO

Left: *Dikembe Mutombo made an instant impact with the Denver Nuggets. His skills as a center caused the team to alter its mad-dash offense in favor of a more controlled attack built around him.*

Below: *Mutombo finished second in the NBA's Rookie of the Year balloting in 1992. He was the fourth overall pick in the 1991 draft after earning All-America and All-Big East Conference honors at Georgetown.*

Position: Center   **Birth Date:** June 25, 1966
College: Georgetown   **Height:** 7' 2"
Drafted: Denver, 1st Rd. ('91)   **Weight:** 245

No one really had a good handle on Dikembe Mutombo's basketball skills when he was picked in the first round of the 1991 draft by the Denver Nuggets. There is no doubting his skills now. He has become the best shot-blocker in the NBA and one of its top rebounders.

Mutombo dominates the low post against Denver opponents. In 1996, he became the first player ever to lead the NBA in blocked shots for three consecutive seasons – and the only player ever to amass more than 300 three years in a row – with 332, just four under his team record of 336. Dikembe had a career-best average of 4.49 per game. In 38 games during the 1996 season, he blocked more shots himself than the entire opposing team.

He also has become a prodigious rebounder, finishing third in the NBA in 1996 with nearly 12 a game on 622 blocks. In just five NBA seasons, Mutombo now ranks seventh in rebounds among all active players, and he is third on the Nuggets' all-time list. He tied a club record with 31 rebounds against Charlotte, the league's highest single-game total since 1994. During the 1996 season, he led the team in rebounding 51 times.

Mutombo has scored more than 5,000 points during his career and was named to his third All-Star Game in 1996. He signed with the Atlanta Hawks after the 1996 season.

His .569 field goal percentage in 1994 was the fourth highest ever by a Nuggets player. "You've got to double team him down low," says one NBA coach, "or he'll dunk you to death."

Above: *Mutombo's full name is Dikembe Mutombo Mpolondo Mukamba Jean Jacque Wamutombo.*

Left: *Mutombo is a relative "basketball baby". He didn't begin playing the sport in his native Zaire until he was 17 years old.*

Page 72: *Dikembe Mutombo became the NBA's most prolific shot-blocker by his fourth season when, in 38 games during the 1996 season, he blocked more shots himself than the entire opposing team. In 1996, he also became the first NBA player ever to lead the league for three consecutive seasons. Mutombo signed with the Atlanta Hawks after the 1996 season.*

HAKEEM OLAJUWON

Hakeem Olajuwon
GQ's "NBA All-Star Style Team"

Position: Center   **Birth Date:** Jan. 21, 1963
College: University of Houston   **Height:** 7' 0"
Drafted: Houston, 1st Rd. ('84)   **Weight:** 250

Translate Hakeem Olajuwon's name into English and it means: "Always being on top."

How appropriate, because that's where Olajuwon found himself after leading his Houston Rockets to consecutive NBA championships in 1994 and 1995, including a four-game sweep of Orlando in 1995. He won his second straight playoff MVP award in 1995 after being the first player in NBA history to be selected as the league's MVP, its Defensive Player of the Year and the MVP of the playoffs in 1994.

Olajuwon has been a force in the NBA since he was a rookie, and he shows no signs of slowing down after a dozen NBA seasons. From 1994 through 1996, Olajuwon averaged 27 points, 11 boards and 3 blocked shots per game. Among other career achievements are his 11 con-

Above: *Hakeem Olajuwon is a perennial All-NBA selection and was named Southwest Conference Player of the Eighties.*

Right: *He finished second to the Bulls' Michael Jordan in Rookie of the Year balloting in 1985.*

Page 74: *Olajuwon has averaged more than 12 rebounds per game throughout his NBA career, and is a regular on the NBA's All-Defensive team each season. He also leads his team in blocked shots, and led the NBA three times.*

Page 75: *Olajuwon was the third NBA player to record 10,000 points, 5,000 rebounds and 1,000 steals, leading his team in steals nine of ten seasons.*

Above: *Olajuwon and Ewing in the 1994 NBA Finals.*

Above right: *1994 NBA MVP Olajuwon.*

secutive seasons with 200 blocked shots and 100 steals and scoring in double figures in 892 of his 900 games.

Olajuwon owns several records:
• All-time NBA blocked shots leader.
• All-time Rockets leader in 12 different categories, including scoring, rebounds, blocked shots, steals and minutes played.
• Only Rockets player ever to grab 10,000 rebounds.

He capped another fine season in 1996 by scoring his 20,000th point and grabbing his 11,000th rebound, and he ranks ninth all-time in both categories. Born in Nigeria, he has become a United States citizen and was a member of America's Dream Team III for the 1996 Olympic Games.

Olajuwon has set himself apart from most centers in NBA history. He is one of just 14 players to average more than 20 points and 10 rebounds; and in 1989, he became the first player ever to have 200+ blocks and steals in the same season. He also became the third player in NBA history ever to exceed 10,000 points, 5,000 rebounds and 1,000 steals, assists and blocks (Kareem Abdul-Jabbar and Julius Erving are the others); and he is the only player to rank among the Top Ten in scoring, rebounding, steals and blocked shots over a three-season span (1987-90).

He has led the Rockets in scoring and blocked shots every season. He has been named to the Western Conference All-Star team for ten seasons, and has been a starter six times. He was the game's MVP in 1994.

The Houston Rockets won a coin flip with the Portland Trail Blazers for the number one pick in the 1984 draft, and picked the seven-foot Olajuwon. He had led the University of Houston team to three consecutive NCAA Final Four appearances. That was remarkable in itself because Olajuwon, a native of Lagos, Nigeria, had never even played basketball until he was 17 years old. He came to the United States and was an immediate star with Houston's famed "Phi Slama Jama" team. Olajuwon later was selected as Player of the Eighties in the Southwest Conference after leading his team to an 88-16 record in three seasons.

He averaged 20.6 points per game in his rookie NBA season and was runner-up to Michael Jordan for Rookie of the Year.

SHAQUILLE O'NEAL

Position: Center
College: LSU
Drafted: Orlando, 1st Rd. ('92)

Birth Date: Mar. 6, 1972
Height: 7' 1"
Weight: 301

The "Shaq Attack" is one of the most terrorizing forms of warfare in the NBA. It has shattered and sent crashing to the floor steel-supported backboards as well as numerous tall centers and other human intruders into a domain on the basketball court that Shaquille O'Neal wants to call his own.

No rookie since Michael Jordan, in 1985, ever made a bigger impact. He became the first rookie to make the All-Star team since Jordan. He won the NBA's scoring title in 1995 with a 29.3 average, after finishing second in 1994. Shaq also led the Magic to the NBA Finals for the first time in 1995. Though his team was swept by Houston in four games, he marked himself as one of the NBA's most dominant players.

Above: *Shaquille O'Neal, who left LSU a year early to play in the NBA, was one of the most publicized rookies in the league's history. He had signed millions of dollars worth of endorsement contracts even before he played his first game. He lived up to most of the hype that preceded him into the pros, and was acclaimed 1993 NBA Rookie of the Year. Following the 1996 season he signed with the Lakers for $121 million.*

Left: *O'Neal's dominance around the basket helped him lead the Orlando Magic in scoring during his first four seasons. His 58 percent field goal shooting average ranks among the top five in the league. He also ranks among the top ten in scoring, rebounding and blocked shots.*

Left: *O'Neal is physically awesome, standing 7' 1" and weighing over 300 pounds. He surprised many in the NBA with his durability over a long 82-game schedule, more than twice what he had played during his LSU seasons.*

Opposite: *A Shaq Attack is an awesome thing to behold. During his first four seasons, O'Neal has been credited with over 1,200 dunks, most of them of the "thunder" variety which have shattered glass backboards on several occasions.*

Thanks to him, the Magic sold out every home game, and on the road he made the Magic second only to Jordan and the Bulls in attracting fans. The first time O'Neal appeared on national TV, in a game against the Phoenix Suns, he dunked a shot with such force that the backboard glass shattered and the cantilevered arm supporting the backboard buckled and collapsed. The next time he was on television, he led the Magic to a triple overtime win over the New York Knicks, prompting a network television executive to note: "One week he stops the network for 35 minutes while the backboard was being repaired, and the next he gives us the first triple-overtime game in network TV in 17 years."

No wonder he wears a tattoo on his right biceps showing a globe palmed by a massive hand, encircled by four words: *THE WORLD IS MINE.*

Shaq also is one of the NBA's most dominant marketing symbols. He earns more than $70 million a year, including his basketball salary, for being involved in a variety of commercial ventures that include a candy bar, a chewy health bar, a video game, a toy figurine, a Disney movie and a rap album as well as shoes, soft drinks and clothing.

Shaq has typically handled the tremendous publicity and commercial pressures incurred by his popularity with aplomb beyond his years. This maturity is a tribute to his solid upbringing by his parents, who only reluctantly allowed him to leave college a year early to sign a pro contract worth more than $40 million – with the promise that he would get his degree regardless of how much money he makes or what his schedule may be.

O'Neal, the son of an Army sergeant, first attracted the attention of a visiting coach from Louisiana State University at age 14 when he was living in Germany where his father was stationed. A year later, he was the most sought after high school player in the country. He chose LSU, where he was an All-America selection during all three varsity seasons.

In every way, O'Neal is no ordinary basketball player. Physically he is awesome: he is 7' 1", weighs 301 pounds and wears size 20 sneakers and a size 24 shirt. The two centers to whom he is often compared, 7' 1" Wilt Chamberlain, the great Hall of Famer of the 1960s and 1970s, and 7' 2" Kareem Abdul-Jabbar, were some 30 pounds lighter.

O'Neal has begun to change the minds of some in pro basketball who say the era of dominant centers is over. He combines an amazing array of power, size and quickness, and even with an almost unprecedented amount of hype about his talent, he has held his own against veteran centers eager to test him.

O'Neal was a unanimous choice as 1993 Rookie of the Year when he broke the Magic's season record for blocked shots before the All-Star break, and owned the career mark before the end of the season. He took the Magic to the playoffs for the first time in his second season and to the NBA Finals in his third year.

During each of his first four NBA seasons, his averages in scoring, rebounding, blocked shots and field goal percentage have been among the league's ten best.

In 1994, he had eight 40-point games and in 1996, he scored more than 30 points 19 times, despite missing almost a third of the season with an injury. He also made his fourth All-Star Game appearance in 1996 and led all scorers with 25 points. In 1994, he won a gold medal on the U.S. Dream Team II in the World Basketball Championships and was voted the MVP of the series, and he also played on the U.S. Dream Team III in Atlanta in the 1996 Olympic Games.

But what topped it all? According to a nationwide poll of 11- to 17-year olds, he was once named Coolest Person Alive.

Below: O'Neal and Denver's Dikembe Mutombo, two of the NBA's best young centers, battle each other in a game between the Nuggets and the Magic. O'Neal's play, along with that of young centers like Mutombo, Alonzo Mourning and David Robinson, drew attention to the role of a dominating center.

GARY PAYTON

Position: Guard   **Birth Date:** July 23, 1968
College: Oregon State   **Height:** 6' 4"
Drafted: Seattle, 1st Rd. ('90)   **Weight:** 190

During the 1996 NBA playoffs, Gary Payton of the Seattle Supersonics gave a vivid display of why he has become one of the league's best all-around guards. He did a very credible job whenever he guarded league and playoff MVP Michael Jordan of the Chicago Bulls. He was responsible for holding him in check when the Sonics made their brief comeback to win two consecutive games.

After the 1996 season, he became the first Seattle player ever named as the NBA's Defensive Player of the Year and he made the NBA's All-Defensive team for the third consecutive year. Part of the reason was his league-leading 231 steals and 2.85 average per game. He also helped the Sonics to become the first NBA team ever to lead the league in steals for four consecutive seasons.

Payton's defensive prowess was one of the biggest reasons why the Seattle Supersonics made him their top pick in 1990 – the second player taken in the draft, and the highest pick in the team's history.

Payton was Oregon State's all-time leading scorer when he left in 1990, and as his NBA career has evolved he has become a scoring threat as well. Payton, who also finished his collegiate competition as the NCAA's all-time number two steal-maker, has lived up to his promise of becoming a multi-faceted NBA star by polishing every aspect of his game during his first five NBA seasons. During the 1996 season, for example, in addition to his great defensive contribution, he averaged nearly 20 points a game and was tenth in the NBA with his seven and a half assists per game. He was selected to the All-NBA second team.

Payton also is one of the NBA's top trash-talkers who often seems to take as much delight in his verbal confrontations as he does in his man-for-man, on-court matchups. He uses his mouth as a defensive weapon because opponents handling the ball often become so dis-tracted by his taunts that they become easy prey for his ability to make steals. And he does it regardless of an opponents's status as he demonstrated during the 1996 NBA Finals when he and superstar Michael Jordan of the Chicago Bulls had several run-ins.

On the other hand, he has mastered the art of the reverse trash-talker who also keeps up a constant barrage of verbal "smack" when he is handling the ball while unerringly dishing out assists to his teammates. Payton has accumulated nearly 3,000 assists during his first five NBA seasons and now averages six per game. He is also an extremely durable player, missing just two games in his first five seasons.

Left: *Gary Payton climaxed the 1996 season by being named to the Dream Team III basketball team that represented the United States in the 1996 Olympic Games in Atlanta.*

SCOTTIE PIPPEN

Position: Forward   **Birth Date:** Sept. 25, 1965
College: Central Arkansas   **Height:** 6' 7"
Drafted: Seattle, 1st Rd. ('87)   **Weight:** 210

There were many who thought Scottie Pippen would become just an "ordinary" player when Michael Jordan retired after leading the Chicago Bulls to their third straight NBA title in 1993.

It didn't happen. Pippen took up the slack left by Jordan's absence – to the extent that was possible – and helped keep Chicago a contender until Jordan returned late in the 1995 season. In 1996, they resumed their dynamic one-two punch by helping the Bulls to win a fourth NBA championship in six years. By that time, there was no denying that Pippen had become one of the NBA's greatest players in his own right. He again was a first team selection on both the All-NBA team and the All-NBA Defensive team. Even with Jordan's greatness, the Bulls

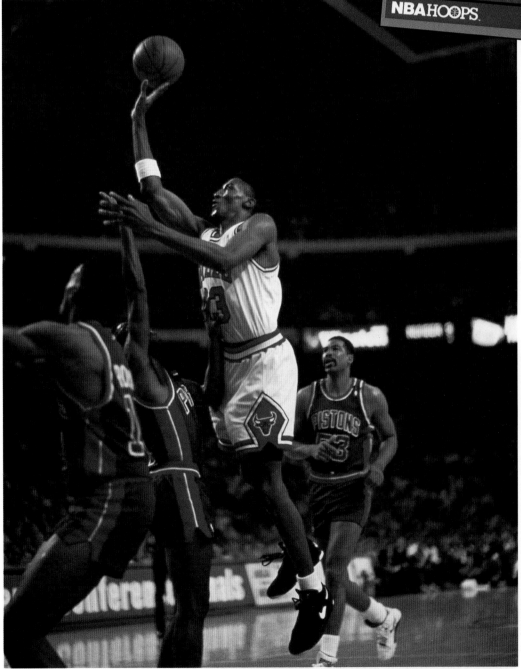

Above: *Scottie Pippen is one of the NBA's top forwards, and many believe he will reach Jordan's plateau before his career ends.*

Left: *Pippen's talents are so prolific that he has created a new position in the NBA – "point forward" – the benchmark for the modern all-purpose basketball player. He also has become an annual pick to the All-NBA team and the All-NBA Defensive team.*

would be hard pressed to duplicate their success without Pippen, who came to them when Jordan insisted the team get better players.

Pippen was a No. 1 draft choice of the Seattle Supersonics in 1987, but he was swapped for Chicago's No.1 choice, Olden Polynice.

As a high school senior, Pippen was 6' 1H" and wasn't given much encouragement when he was accepted at Central Arkansas. By the time he arrived, he had grown two inches. He then added 20 pounds and grew another 3" to stand at 6' 7" by the end of his senior season.

"He took the skills he had learned as a small player and used them when he was bigger," one of his college coaches noted. "His arms are so long and his hands so big that he really plays like someone who is 6' 10" or 6' 11"."

With that package, the Bulls had one of the key players who eventually brought them four NBA championships, and a player who became a star in his own right. Opponents found they could not expend all of their defensive energy trying to stop Jordan because Pippen was capable of producing big scoring games.

Said Bulls coach Phil Jackson, "Right from the start,

he could rebound yet still dribble the length of the court. He could post up and he had those slashing sorts of moves. You knew he could become a very good player, but you didn't know how good. He played a few times at guard in his first couple of seasons, bringing the ball up against teams with pressing guards. But mostly we used him at small forward."

"As more and more teams pressed, we wound up with Michael bringing up the ball and we didn't want to do that. So Scottie became a third ball advancer as part of an offense that attacked at multiple points. From that

position, he started being able to take control, to make decisions. He became a bit of everything."

Pippen is tall enough and jumps high enough to move inside. He handles the ball well enough to play guard if needed, but also is a "point forward," a position that he created for himself. Guard him high, and he takes the defender low; guard him low, and he can go high and shoot. Leave him alone for a moment and he is gone, soaring for a stuff shot that is more reminiscent of the moves Julius (Dr. J.) Erving used to make than those patented by Michael Jordan.

MARK PRICE

Position: Guard
College: Georgia Tech
Drafted: Dallas, 2nd Rd. ('86)

Birth Date: Feb. 16, 1964
Height: 6' 1"
Weight: 170

Mark Price has long been the master of running the pick-and-roll play. He uses his quickness and skill driving to the basket. "No one runs the pick-and-roll better," notes one former NBA executive. "Price will come off a screen at any time, and after he catches the ball, his teammate will turn and set up for an immediate pick-and-roll."

Price had to learn this skill after he had been a "shooting" guard at Georgia Tech. In fact, the Dallas Maver-

icks had second thoughts about his ability after picking him on the second round of the 1986 draft, and immediately traded him to Cleveland.

Price played nine seasons with the Cleveland Cavaliers before being traded to the Washington Bullets before the 1996 season. He was sidelined with a broken foot for most of the season, and went to the Golden State Warriors at season's end.

During his seasons with Cleveland, he was consistently among the NBA's assists leaders, and is the Cavaliers' all-time leader in free throw accuracy, steals, assists and three-point field goals and accuracy.

DINO RADJA

Position: Forward   **Birth Date:** Apr. 24, 1967
College: None   **Height:** 6' 1"
Drafted: Boston, 2nd Rd. ('89)   **Weight:** 225

It took a while – a long while by NBA standards – but the Celtics finally lured Dino Radja from Yugoslavia, and he has since become their most productive player. Radja flirted with the Celtics while he played in Italy for three seasons where he was a consistent 20-point scorer, and he teamed with current Chicago Bulls forward Toni Kukoc to help their national team to win silver medals in the 1988 and 1992 Olympic Games.

Like all European players who transfer to the NBA, it took Radja a season to upgrade his game to the NBA's exacting level. In his first NBA season, 1994, he averaged 15 points per game, but not accustomed to the NBA he sometimes fell prey to the rough-and-tumble play under the boards and disappeared altogether from the scoring charts.

In 1995 the hard work Radja put in between seasons paid off, and he has continued to improve his overall game. He has become the Celtics' leading scorer and needs only to upgrade his all-around defensive play to fulfill the promise that the Celtics believed would make him one of their top players.

"Dino has always given us a big lift at key times," notes M.L. Carr, Celtics head coach, "and that is a sign that he has begun to reach the level we had long anticipated, given his fine talent."

Left: *Dino Radja was a European star and two-time Olympian before joining the Boston Celtics. He has averaged more than 16 points per game since coming to the NBA.*

Above: *Radja has worked to strengthen his game since joining the Celtics, and he even has taken himself out of the lineup when he believes he is not playing at a high level.*

MAHMOUD ABDUL RAUF
(Chris Jackson)

Position: Guard
College: LSU
Drafted: Denver, 1st Rd. ('90)

Birth Date: Mar. 9, 1969
Height: 6' 1"
Weight: 165

Mahmoud Abdul Rauf, known as Chris Jackson before becoming a Muslim in 1993, has become the NBA's leading free throw shooter, and one of its ablest three-point marksmen. As a Denver Nuggets' guard, he won his second free throw shooting title in 1996, with a .930 accuracy mark – he missed just 11 of the 157 foul shots he attempted. He was traded to the Sacramento Kings after the 1996 season.

Abdul-Rauf, who has scored more than 7,000 points during his NBA career, hit seven of eight three-pointers in one 1996 game – one of three times during that season when he canned seven three-pointers. He also led Denver in scoring for the fourth consecutive season, the first Denver player ever to achieve that mark, while matching his career high of 19.1 points per game.

The third choice in the 1990 NBA draft, he was the Denver Nuggets' highest draft choice ever when he left Louisiana State University after a star-studded sophomore year. It turned out that he had left too soon, because he got caught in a maze of immaturity and bad basketball habits and set his career on the brink of failure after his first two NBA seasons.

After the 1992 season, he took stock of himself and didn't like what he saw. "I wasn't satisfied with myself the first two years, and I was hearing a lot of things, reading a lot of things that disappointed myself," he said. "So I changed. I wanted to prove to myself that I could play in the NBA because if that happened, then others would be convinced also."

And change he did. In 1993, his third season, he raised his scoring average seven points a game while leading his team in every major scoring statistic. He also had a couple of eye-popping moments, once beating Sacramento with a 55-foot three-point shot at the buzzer, and finishing the season with another last-second, game-winning three-pointer against Phoenix.

Left: *When Mahmoud Abdul Rauf/Chris Jackson finally got his act together in 1993, he nearly matched his NBA point totals for his first two seasons combined. He was traded to the Sacramento Kings after the 1996 season.*

GLEN RICE

Position: Forward
College: Michigan
Drafted: Miami, 1st Rd. ('89)

Birth Date: May 28, 1967
Height: 6' 8"
Weight: 220

After helping Michigan to the NCAA championship in 1989, Glen Rice came to the NBA and got the reputation of being a "tweener," a player deemed not good enough to play at one position full time during his first couple of seasons with the Miami Heat. But he established himself with the Miami Heat at the "small forward" position and became such a star that in order for Miami to get all-star center Alonzo Mourning in a multiplayer trade with Charlotte before the 1996 season, they

had to make him part of the deal.

With Charlotte, Rice has teamed with Larry Johnson to form one of the NBA's best "dynamic duos" – they were eighth in combined scoring in 1996 with more than 42 points per game and led the Hornets in scoring 72 times. Each scored 20 or more points in 47 games.

Rice became the Miami Heat's all-time single season scorer in 1992, as well as the team's MVP. Most importantly, he became a more efficient, two-pronged offensive player. He still is a fine three-point shooter, so if the defense lays off, he fires from the outside; if it crowds him, he is quick enough to work a pick-and-roll, or drive past a defender to the basket.

MITCH RICHMOND

Position: Guard   **Birth Date:** June 30, 1965
College: Kansas State   **Height:** 6' 5"
Drafted: Golden State, 1st Rd. ('88)   **Weight:** 215

Mitch Richmond is a worker – and an achiever. His career high 1,872 points during the 1996 season made him only the seventh player in NBA history to average more than 21 points in each of his first eight seasons. During the 1996 season, Mitch also was named to his fourth straight NBA All-Star Game; and he gained a berth on the 1996 U.S. Olympic Dream Team III. No wonder the Sacramento Kings parted with No. 1 pick Billy Owens, the third player picked in the 1992 draft, to get him from the Golden State Warriors.

Richmond raised himself from a mediocre player in junior college to become an All-America at Kansas State, and was the only unanimous selection to the NBA's all-rookie team in 1989 after averaging 22 points per game.

But working to improve is the story of Richmond's basketball life. "I enjoy the stress and pressure of playing," he commented, "and of having my teammates rely on me."

In 1994, Richmond became the first Kings player since Otis Birdsong in 1981 to earn all-league honors; his 23 point average was the highest since Birdsong hit 24.6 in 1981. He was chosen the All-Star Game MVP in 1995.

Left: *Mitch Richmond won NBA Rookie of the Year honors in 1989, and then became the first winner since Phil Ford, in 1979, to improve his scoring average in each of the next two seasons. He also ranked among the NBA's top 20 scorers in each of his first five seasons. "I think we're very similiar in styles," Michael Jordan of the Chicago Bulls once noted of Richmond. He has scored more than 10,000 points and handed out more than 2,000 assists.*

ISAIAH RIDER

Position: Guard
College: UNLV
Drafted: Minnesota, 1st Rd. ('93)

Birth Date: Mar. 12, 1971
Height: 6' 5"
Weight: 215

Isaiah Rider, nicknamed J.R., is one of the NBA's bright, new, up-tempo players who reminded many of the late Pete Maravich when he came into the league in the 1970s. He still must refine his overall game and get a steely-eyed approach to the NBA style. But many believe Rider may have been limited by the Timberwolves, and may fare better with the well-established Trail Blazers, to whom he was traded after the 1996 season. In 1996, after his third season, he already had scored more than 4,000 points, handed out 500 assists and was

Minnesota's all-time leader in three-point field goals.

Rider plays with the same all-motion style as Maravich did, constantly moving at top speed. While not yet as adept at handling the ball, Rider is a whirling dervish when he heads for the basket, renowned for his no-look passes and fancy dribbling. He has also begun to tailor his flashy style to become more consistent.

As a rookie, Rider made himself known when he predicted he would win the NBA's Slam Dunk Contest during the 1994 All-Star Game weekend – and he did just that. He then finished off that same season as a starter on the league's all-rookie team. Rider averaged 16 points per game in his rookie season and became the Timberwolves' leading scorer in his second year.

CLIFF ROBINSON

Position: Forward
College: Connecticut
Drafted: Portland, 2nd Rd. ('89)

Birth Date: Dec. 16, 1966
Height: 6' 10"
Weight: 225

Cliff Robinson is an all-purpose player who has worked tirelessly at his job, seemingly without much notice until he suddenly blossomed into an All-Star performer.

He came to the Trail Blazers as a second round pick from the University of Connecticut, where he was the only player in that school's history to score more than 600 points in two different seasons.

Most NBA observers feel that Robinson is a natural small forward, but most of his starts have been at center, earning the team a winning record. In his rookie season, he played more minutes than any first year Trail Blazer since Sam Bowie in 1985, and for most of his first four NBA seasons he was the first player off the bench. His reserve status was celebrated when he was the recipient of the NBA's Sixth Man Award after the 1993 season, during which he also was fifth in balloting as the league's most improved player.

He finally became a permanent starter in the 1994 season, and was rewarded by being named to the NBA All-Star team. He made quite an impact when he scored ten points and added five assists and two rebounds in the mid-season game.

During his time with the Blazers, Robinson has steadily crept up the scoring charts until, in 1994, he finally broke the 20-point average to rank among the NBA's top 20 scorers. During that season, he scored 30 or more points in eight games, and surpassed 20 in 41 games to solidify his role as a starter. He consistently leads the Trail Blazers in scoring at home and on the road. He also has developed into a fine three-point shooter. In 1996 he had a team record 178 three-pointers, and hit at least one in 41 straight games.

Robinson is a fine defensive player. In 1992 he was the first Trail Blazer to block more than 100 shots since Bowie and Mychal Thompson seven years earlier. During the 1994 season he led the team three times with five steals per game.

Robinson is also one of the NBA's most durable players. He set a club record when he played in every regular season and playoff game during his first five seasons, helping Portland to contend for the title in each of those years. He is among the club's top twenty in minutes played, points scored, three-point field goals, rebounds, blocked shots and steals.

Right: *Cliff Robinson first made his reputation in the NBA by coming off the bench for the Portland Trail Blazers, and received the NBA's Sixth Man Award in 1993. He is a fine all-around player, a natural small forward who also has been very effective playing at center.*

Opposite: *Isaiah (J.R.) Rider, who, as a rookie, burst onto the NBA scene in 1994 by winning its annual Slam Dunk Contest after brashly predicting he'd do just that, is a bright, up-tempo player who reminds many of the late Pete Maravich for his whirling-dervish style of play.*

DAVID ROBINSON

Left: *David Robinson is a superb athlete, and while he has been among the NBA leaders in rebounds and blocked shots, he also has averaged 138 steals per season.*

Below: *Robinson was the first player selected in the 1987 draft, and in 1992 he was named to his second U.S. Olympic team. He was NBA Rookie of the Year in 1990, and has played in the NBA All-Star Game every season.*

Opposite top: *David Robinson, nicknamed "The Admiral," is the first player from Navy ever to play in the NBA. He was consensus NCAA Player of the Year in 1987, then served two years of active duty as a naval officer.*

Opposite bottom: *How valuable is David Robinson to the San Antonio Spurs? In 1996, he won the NBA's IBM Award for the fifth time. The award is based on a computerized rating that measures a player's overall contribution to his team. Robinson also has been named to the NBA's All-Defensive team in each of his first seven seasons, four times making the first team.*

Position: Center   **Birth Date:** Aug. 6, 1965
College: U.S. Naval Academy   **Height:** 7' 1"
Drafted: San Antonio, 1st Rd. ('87)   **Weight:** 235

David Robinson – "The Admiral" – set his course to become the NBA's "Center of the 1990s," and he is right on course. He was chosen the NBA's Most Valuable Player in 1995 after leading the San Antonio Spurs to the most wins that season. It was an appropriate follow-up to his pulsating performance on the last day of the 1994 season that brought him the scoring title. He was selected for the NBA All-Star Game and the all-NBA teams in each of his first seven seasons. During these seasons, he has amassed over 14,000 points and 6,000 rebounds.

Robinson scored a career high 71 points in the final regular season game in 1994 against the Los Angeles Clippers to clinch the scoring title by six points over Shaquille O'Neal (2,383 to 2,377). He was runner-up for the NBA's MVP award, and became only the third player in NBA history to be among the top 30 in six major categories.

There is no other NBA center whose game is as well rounded. Here is a look at the post-season honors he has received:

• **1990:** NBA Rookie of the Year; All-Rookie first team; All-NBA Defensive second team; All-NBA third team.
• **1991:** All-NBA first team; All-NBA Defensive first team.
• **1992:** NBA Defensive Player of the Year; All-NBA first team; All-NBA Defensive first team.
• **1993:** All-NBA Defensive second team; All-NBA third team.
• **1994:** All-NBA second team; All-NBA Defensive second team.
• **1995:** NBA MVP and center on All-NBA first team.
• **1996:** All-NBA first team and All-NBA Defensive first team.

What is most amazing is that Robinson didn't start playing basketball until his senior year in high school, and as a freshman at the United States Naval Academy (to which he gained admission on the strength of a 1320 score on his college boards) he averaged just seven points a game.

By his senior year, he had grown seven inches and was the third highest scorer in the nation (28.3 points per game) and fourth highest rebounder (11.8). He was a unanimous All-America selection and was named NCAA Player of the Year.

David was the NBA's first pick in 1987 by the San Antonio Spurs, though he still had to serve two years of active Navy duty.

He was the only rookie in the 1990 All-Star Game and he was named to the gold medal-winning U.S. Dream Team in the 1992 Olympics.

Right: *David Robinson blocked more than 2,000 shots in his first seven seasons with the San Antonio Spurs, and led the NBA in 1991 and 1992.*

Opposite: *"Mr. Robinson's Neighborhood" has taken on a two-fold meaning in the NBA – it is his territory around the basket, and the focal point for his popular anti-drug commercials. Robinson contributes both on the court and off. In 1992 David and his wife Valerie created the David Robinson Foundation which has donated over a million dollars to support family-based programs.*

GLENN ROBINSON

Position: Forward
College: Purdue
Drafted: Milwaukee, 1st Rd. ('94)

Birth Date: Jan. 10, 1973
Height: 6' 8"
Weight: 225

The first time Indiana Pacers coach Larry Brown coached against Glenn Robinson of the Milwaukee Bucks, he said, "He's going to be a great first round pick. Someday, he'll be part of another Dream Team."

In his first two NBA seasons, he scored more than 3,000 points. Robinson and Vin Baker are a deadly combination for the Bucks – they scored more than 43 percent of the team's points in 1996, the second best tandem in the NBA that season and the second best in the team's history.

After roaring out of Purdue University where he was college basketball's Player of the Year in 1994, Robinson has a lot to live up to in the NBA – $68.15 million for 10 years, to be exact (down from an original demand of $100 million that Milwaukee Bucks owner Herb Kohl said was higher than the value of his team).

Robinson soon settled down to prove his worth. He was named the NBA's Rookie of the Month after less than two months in the league when he averaged nearly 22 points, seven rebounds and two assists over a 15-game stretch. He led his team in scoring in eight of those games and had 20 or more points in 11 of them.

In his first game against the Orlando Magic that features such talents as Shaquille O'Neal, Horace Grant, Anfernee Hardaway and Nick Anderson, Robinson played 36 minutes and scored 25 points, added four rebounds, made six assists, had two steals and just four turnovers. "He never saw so much talent on one side of the ball at Purdue," noted one observer, "and when he got double-teamed, it rattled him a little. But he knew how to fight through it and he's only going to get better with more experience."

Left: *Glenn Robinson was the 1994 College Player of the Year during an All-America season at Purdue, and he was the first player chosen in that year's NBA draft. He began to make his mark in the NBA by being selected as Player of the Month less than two months after playing his first game. He signed a contract for more than $68 million after first demanding $100 million from the Milwaukee Bucks.*

Opposite: *Robinson's nickname is "Big Dog". He says that the biggest pressure he faces in the NBA is the feeling "that I have to win. I never fear living up to the big contract. As long as you play hard, that's all you can ask."*

Ex-Milwaukee coach Mike Dunleavy believes it will take Robinson a few years to live up to the great expectations that he has set for himself with his outrageous salary demands and his huge final settlement. "By that time," Dunleavy said, "he should be doing what people expect."

Robinson plays well inside and out. One of his most noticeable qualities, his tenacity, was noted by one of his college coaches, Bruce Weber: "He'll play until he destroys somebody." He has displayed fine passing skills to go along with his scoring, and quick hands make him a ball hawk on defense. He is also very aggressive when taking the ball to the basket – and has thus earned his nickname as "Big Dog".

"I just want to play hard. I want to be the best," Robinson says. "Then good things will happen. I'm getting better and better every game." That fact was already borne out before his rookie season had ended when opposing teams began to double-team him – the ultimate respect for a feared player.

DETLEF SCHREMPF

Position: Forward
College: Washington
Drafted: Dallas, 1st Rd. ('85)

Birth Date: Jan. 21, 1963
Height: 6' 10"
Weight: 230

When Detlef Schrempf was injured while playing soccer in his native Germany at the age of 12, he gave up the sport for a while and began playing basketball. As a result, the game of soccer may have lost a budding star but the NBA eventually gained one of the best – and most versatile – European players it has ever signed.

In 1993, Schrempf became the first European player ever named to the NBA All-Star team, a fitting reward for someone who has played every position and proven his versatility by twice winning the NBA's Sixth Man Award.

Schrempf was a star at the University of Washington, where he played all five positions. His Huskies coach, Marv Harshman, called him the best player he ever coached. A first-round draft pick of the Dallas Mavericks in 1985, he struggled to find his NBA niche and was

traded in 1989 to the Indiana Pacers. He played both forward positions, center and even guard for the Pacers for four and a half seasons before being traded to the Seattle Supersonics before the 1994 season. He was a perfect fit with the Sonics, leading them in scoring 15 times and in rebounding eight times as they forged the NBA's best record.

"I was asked to do different things at Indiana, play various positions," Schrempf said. "As a result, I can take a rebound and dribble it down the court, creating something offensively. I do not just stand around and watch."

Former Indiana coach Bob Hill commented: "He does all the right things away from the court, and then comes in and practices as hard as he plays. He works better up front because he is quicker and more mobile than most big forwards."

Schrempf remains a citizen of his native country, and played on Germany's Olympic basketball team in 1984 and 1992.

Left: *Detlef Schrempf, who went from the Indiana Pacers to the Seattle Supersonics in a 1993 trade for Derrick McKey and Gerald Paddio, has teamed with Shawn Kemp to give the Supersonics a formidable front court, and together they average nearly 40 points and 10 rebounds per game.*

RIK SMITS

Position: Center
College: Marist
Drafted: Indiana, 1st Rd. ('88)

Birth Date: Aug. 23, 1966
Height: 7' 4"
Weight: 265

Rik Smits, whose nickname is "The Dunking Dutchman" because he was born in Eindhoven, Holland, became a true force as a center for the Indiana Pacers during the last half of the 1994 season when he averaged nearly 18 points per game and helped send the team to the finals in the Eastern Conference playoffs.

He has built on that performance and now has become an excellent all-around force for the Indiana Pacers. Smits averaged 18.5 points, best of his career, in 1996, and led the team in scoring 29 times. He scored in double figures 59 of his 63 games and has now passed the 9,000-point mark in career scoring. He also has accumulated a total of more than 3,500 rebounds.

Smits has lived up to the high expectations held for him ever since 1988 when he was a Number 1 draft pick from Marist College in Poughkeepsie, N.Y., where he was the East Coast Athletic Conference Metro Player of the Year in his last two seasons; and he was also chosen the school's player of the decade.

Smits is 7' 4" and 265 pounds but because of his lack of top-flight college competition, other NBA centers took advantage of his inexperience and forced him to work hard to elevate his game. Smits was prone to foul before learning to use his great size to become more dominating as an inside player. In fact, he led the NBA in disqualifications in his first two seasons, but he learned his lessons well and is now only the second Pacer ever to block more than 700 shots.

Left: *Rik Smits, a native of Eindhoven, Holland, helped the Indiana Pacers into the playoffs in seven of his first eight seasons and he has averaged double figures during each of his NBA seasons.*

101

LATRELL SPREWELL

Position: Guard   **Birth Date:** Sept. 8, 1970
College: Alabama   **Height:** 6' 5"
Drafted: Golden State, 1st Rd. ('92)   **Weight:** 190

Latrell Sprewell (pronounced Luh-TRELL SPREE-well) is such a great talent that the only way to determine how far he will go in the NBA is to watch how he devotes himself to all facets of the game – on and off the court.

Sprewell has gone from "Latrell Who?" status when he was initially drafted by the Warriors in 1992 after just two varsity seasons at Alabama, to being the first guard in Warriors history – and the youngest in the NBA in ten years – to be named to the All-NBA first team at the end of his second season.

He also made the All-Star Game for the first time that year, and is continuing to improve his game. His biggest problem – easily solvable with more mental discipline – is adhering to the rules set down by his coaches. Former Warriors coach Don Nelson, with whom Sprewell had a celebrated run in, once said, "The sky is the absolute limit for Latrell Sprewell."

When his mind is on the game – which is most of the time – Sprewell is a start-to-finish player. One of his many great qualities is his stamina. Sprewell had set a record for minutes played at Alabama and has consistently averaged an impressive 40 minutes a game for the Golden State Warriors.

Offensively, he continues to steadily improve his game, raising his average from 15 points per game to being a consistent 20 points per game scorer, from his rookie to his third season. In 1994, he also became the youngest Warrior ever to lead the team in scoring, and continues to be the team's scoring leader. Interestingly, he consistently outshoots the opposing shooting guard, and in 1996 he led the Warriors team in scoring more than 35 times.

Sprewell is also very adept at defense. He was the youngest player ever selected for the NBA's All-Defensive team when the league's coaches named him to the second team after the 1994 season. He soon will break the 1,000 mark in defensive rebounds.

When he played a 1995 season game against the perennial all-pro guard Clyde Drexler, who had a 24-point scoring average, he helped to limit him to 13 points. He also leads the Warriors in steals and is among the NBA's top 20 players in that department.

"Next to Michael Jordan," said Indiana Pacers' all-pro guard Reggie Miller, "He has got to be the quickest two-guard with the ball that I have ever played against. He can shoot, run the floor, jump, and he doesn't get tired."

Latrell Sprewell was one of the youngest guards in NBA history to make the All-NBA first team, in 1994.

Left: *Sprewell was the youngest player ever named to the NBA's All-Defensive team, after the 1994 season, and now leads his team in steals.*

Opposite: *Sprewell had played just two varsity seasons at Alabama before coming to Golden State. His hard work to improve his shooting has made him the Warriors' top scorer.*

JOHN STARKS

Position: Guard
College: Oklahoma State
Drafted: Free Agent, Golden St. ('88)

Birth Date: Aug. 10, 1965
Height: 6' 5"
Weight: 185

John Starks is the ultimate rags-to-riches story: a player who came from the bush leagues to a key starting role on an NBA title contender where he is its best outside shooter and its emotional engine.

Starks was signed as a free agent by the Golden State Warriors in 1988 after one season at Oklahoma State. He played only sparingly in the 1989 season, and the next season was sent to Cedar Rapids of the Continental Basketball Association where he played for $500 a month, supplementing his income by working at a loading dock and bagging groceries. That summer, he played basketball at Memphis in the even more obscure World Basketball League before the Knicks signed him as a "prac-

tice player" prior to the 1991 season.

Even then, it took one last desperate act to save his basketball career. Knowing he was about to be cut and deciding to go out with a bang, he tried to make a thunderous dunk over center Patrick Ewing in a scrimmage, only to be swatted to the floor, where he sustained a leg injury that forced New York to keep him until he was healed. When that happened, the Knicks suddenly needed a player, and this time around, Starks' basketball dream was realized.

He has proved his NBA ability as the Knicks' shooting guard, and he has become the Knicks' No. 2 scorer behind Patrick Ewing. He has become the Knicks' all-time three-point shooter in playoff competition and ranks behind Danny Ainge in all-time NBA statistics. He also is the Knicks' No.2 assist-maker in the playoffs, behind Hall of Famer Walt Frazier.

Left: *John Starks was not drafted by any NBA team when he finished college, and he worked his way through basketball's minor leagues before the Golden State Warriors signed him as a free agent. When the Warriors released him the Knicks picked him up, and he has become their workhorse backcourt player with his playmaking abilities and three-point shots.*

JOHN STOCKTON

Position: Guard
College: Gonzaga
Drafted: Utah, 1st Rd. ('84)

Birth Date: Mar. 26, 1962
Height: 6' 1"
Weight: 175

John Stockton has the fastest hands in the West – the NBA's Western Conference, that is. Stockton, the pro guard of the Utah Jazz, is the NBA's all-time leader in both assists and steals. In 1995, he passed both Magic Johnson and Oscar Robertson to establish the assists record; and in 1996, he broke Maurice Cheeks' steals mark. He has more than 11,300 assists and 2,365 steals.

Stockton is a perennial choice for the All-Star Game and the All-NBA team. He also reprised his 1992 U.S. Olympic Dream Team appearance by being named to Dream Team III for the 1996 Games.

Stockton has played in 980 of a possible 984 games during his career and has accumulated more than 1,000 assists during a season seven times. He has led the NBA nine times and set the single-season record of 1,164 in 1991.

Right: *John Stockton was named to the 1992 and 1996 U.S. Olympic teams.*

Below: *Stockton is tough on defense, and is an all-time leader in steals.*

JOHN STOCKTON

He runs the offense of the Utah Jazz as a conductor directs his musicians. He is very adept at setting up players for open shots, getting the ball to them at the right spot and at the right time.

When he first joined the Jazz, Stockton's reputation was forged on his playmaking ability. But he is also a consistent double-figure scorer. Play him too tightly and he will dump the ball to a shooter; back off and he has enough quickness to dart through an opening and score.

What impresses teammates and foes alike is Stockton's total dedication to helping his team. "That's the kind of person he's been since he started to play for the Jazz," says his coach Jerry Sloan. "That's why the other players like to play with him. He's a willing giver to this game and to his teammates, and you can't take those things lightly."

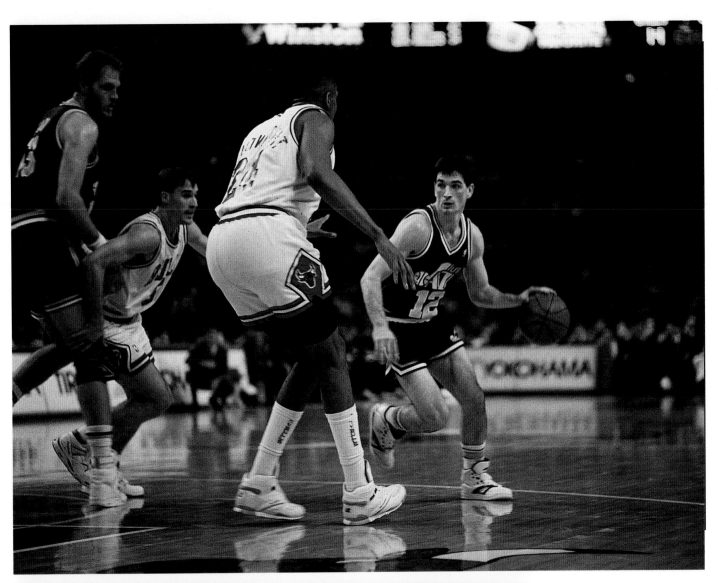

Opposite: *Many in the NBA believe that John Stockton and Karl Malone are the best guard-forward tandem in the NBA.*

Above: *Stockton is masterful in the way that he directs Utah's offense, particularly with his trigger-quick passing.*

Left: *Stockton had five consecutive seasons with 1,100 or more assists.*

Page 108: *Stockton's great passing and his ability to steal the ball have overshadowed his good offensive shooting, particularly his ability to move to the basket, or stop and pop a quick jump shot.*

CLARENCE WEATHERSPOON

Position: Forward

College: Southern Mississippi

Drafted: Philadelphia, 1st Rd. ('92)

Birth Date: Sept. 8, 1970

Height: 6' 7"

Weight: 240

Clarence Weatherspoon has the great ability to shoulder a substantial chunk of his team's offensive and defensive load.

Although he is best suited to playing the small forward position, he has willingly done stints as power forward and center – no mean feat for someone who is 6' 7", the size of many NBA guards. In 1996, for the second time in three seasons he was one of five players to hit the NBA's "100 Club" – for those players who get at least 100 points, rebounds, steals, blocks and assists for the season.

When Weatherspoon first came into the NBA in 1993

his defensive skills were considered his forte, but he immediately built up his offensive game and finished by scoring more points in his first two seasons then any player in 76ers history. Clarence set a rookie scoring record in 1993, and in 1996 he became only the third Sixers player to accumulate 5,000 points and 2,500 rebounds during his first four seasons. He also has more than 700 assists in his young career.

The 76ers think so highly of his leadership that they elected him team captain. Despite the team's problems in the 1990s – he has played for three coaches in five seasons – he is consistently among the team's statistical leaders.

Clarence first made his mark at Southern Mississippi University, where he was the first basketball player ever to have his number retired.

CHRIS WEBBER

Position: Forward   **Birth Date:** Mar. 1, 1973
College: Michigan   **Height:** 6' 10"
Drafted: Orlando, 1st Rd. ('93)   **Weight:** 250

In less than two seasons, Chris Webber had already played on three NBA teams. He would have been playing for the University of Michigan during that time if he had not become the first sophomore since Magic Johnson in 1979 to be a first round draft selection.

Webber was drafted by the Orlando Magic in 1993 and then traded to Golden State for three Number 1 draft picks and guard Anfernee Hardaway, whom the Magic had coveted. Webber had a spectacular rookie season with the Warriors before getting into a jam with coach Don Nelson that resulted in his trade to the Washington Bullets in exchange for forward Tom Gugliotta early in the 1995 season.

But his problems at Golden State did not dim his achievements as a rookie when he drew unanimous acclaim as a "can't miss" star.

He won the Rookie of the Year Award after averaging nearly 18 points, nine rebounds, four assists and two blocked shots per game. He was the only rookie in NBA history ever to score 1,000 points, grab 500 rebounds, get 100 assists, 150 blocks and 75 steals in one season.

Webber is still considered a star of the future, despite having missed most of the 1996 season with a broken shoulder.

Left: *Chris Webber was NBA Rookie of the Year in 1994 with the Golden State Warriors after becoming the first rookie in NBA history ever to score 1,000 points, grab 500 rebounds, accumulate 100 assists, block 150 shots and get 75 steals in one season. And after demanding to be traded prior to the 1995 season, he has begun to live up to his "can't miss" star projection with the Washington Bullets.*

DOUG WEST

Position: Guard
College: Villanova
Drafted: Minnesota, 2nd Rd. ('89)

Birth Date: May 27, 1967
Height: 6' 6"
Weight: 200

Doug West arrived in the NBA after setting scoring records at Villanova, and was immediately made a defensive specialist. His first three coaches at Minnesota each used him in a different manner – all with great success. In his early seasons he played alternatively as a shooting guard and point guard, but when the Minnesota Timberwolves drafted Isaiah Rider in 1993, it seemed as though West's starting days might be over.

Instead, he moved to small forward.

West has now become a valuable swing man for the Timberwolves, alternating off the bench between forward and guard. He has produced more than 1,000 assists and is second all-time in steals.

"When people start talking about different guys coming in and taking my spot," he says, "I don't pay any attention. If someone does beat me out, that's fine. I haven't been in a situation where I have been beaten out yet. I am going to compete. I had to guard Michael Jordan for a few years, so nothing else worries me now."

Left: *Doug West is a constant blur of motion during a game, as the Los Angeles Lakers discovered when they tried to stop him on a drive. He is a graceful athlete who was given a top defensive role early in his NBA career before being allowed more offensive responsibilities.*

INDEX